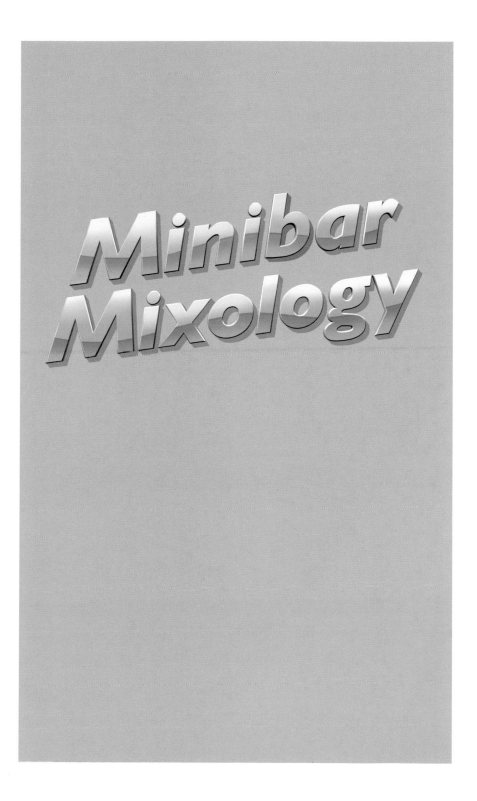

Minibar Mixology

Minibar Mixology

Reed West

Sterling Publishing Co., Inc.
New York

Library of Congress Cataloging-in-Publication Data Available

2 4 6 8 10 9 7 5 3 1

Published by Sterling Publishing Co., Inc.
387 Park Avenue South, New York, NY 10016

© 2006 by Sterling Publishing Co., Inc.

The recipes in this book have been excerpted from the following Sterling titles:
Perfect Cocktails by Marthe Le Van © 2001 by Lark Books
Classic Summer Cocktails, text © 2001 by Salvatore Calabrese
Classic After-Dinner Cocktails © 1999 by Salvatore Calabrese
Salvatore Calabrese's Virgin Cocktails © 2004 by Salvatore Calabrese

Photographs by James Duncan and Evan Bracken
except for page 167 © Corbis
Compiled by Bob Strauss
Book design by Leah Lococo Ltd
Interior Illustrations by Monica Gurevich

Distributed in Canada by Sterling Publishing
C/o Canadian Manda Group, 165 Dufferin Street
Toronto, Ontario, Canada M6K 3H6
Distributed in the United Kingdom by GMC Distribution Services
Castle Place, 166 High Street, Lewes, East Sussex, England BN7 1XU
Distributed in Australia by Capricorn Link (Australia) Pty. Ltd.
P.O. Box 704, Windsor, NSW 2756, Australia

Printed in China
All rights reserved

Sterling ISBN-13: 978-1-4027-2925-6
ISBN-10: 1-4027-2925-1

For information about custom editions, special sales, premium and
corporate purchases, please contact Sterling Special Sales
Department at 800-805-5489 or specialsales@sterlingpub.com.

Contents

INTRODUCTION

Remember way, way back in college, when you had one of those cool mini-fridges in your dorm room that your parents rented for you so you could stock up on whole milk and power bars, but which you crammed full of beer instead? Those were the days. You'd come back from classes, pop open a tall one and catch up on that afternoon's install-ment of your favorite daytime television show; invite your girlfriend over for a late-night carafe of wine, then have her stay over for an intimate breakfast of week-old orange juice and stale Pop Tarts; and power-chug six-packs of the cheapest beer available until the wee dawn hours, then remove the shelves and try to stuff inside whoever passed out first.

Well, cast your hazy reminiscences aside, because there's a grown-up equivalent of the rented dorm-room midget fridge: the hotel minibar. Much swankier than its campus relation, the hotel minibar presents itself to you fully stocked with a cornucopia of food, drink, and assorted goodies: scotch and vodka, pretzels and peanuts, condoms (if you're not staying at a Disneyland resort, that is) and playing cards. And although your parents are unlikely to reimburse you for your minibar splurges (see page 15, "A Brief Word about Expenses"), odds are you're a gainfully employed, well-heeled adult who can afford to indulge himself every once in awhile in a homemade Bloody Mary and a $5 tube of Pringles. (And yes, many of the recipes in this book require you to order from room service, but if you didn't have cash to burn, you'd be staying in a YMCA, right?)

Often taken for granted—if it's noticed at all, that is—the hotel minibar can be an endless fount of entertainment. In this book, you'll learn how to amuse your lonely traveling self with arcane cocktail recipes, cozy up to your significant other with a pitcher of minibar-plus-room-service Pina Coladas (see page 99), pool your resources with everyone else on the floor of your hotel for an all-night minibar bash, and entertain your kids with alcohol-free virgin minibar concoctions. We'll even give you a variety of party games you can play, alone or with others, to add to the minibar-fueled amusement. Every mini-bar has a different stock, and your particular hotel's room service may not be able to provide certain items. Don't despair—substitute a liquor or drink that you have, find another drink, or get creative and mix what you have. Maybe you can create the next hot drink.

Remember, it wouldn't be there if they didn't want you to use it, right? Open up that bar, order something good on pay-per-view, and have fun!

What You'll Find in Your Minibar

Just as the basic chemistry of life can be broken down into 20 amino acids, the components of your average minibar can be broadly divided into three categories: food, drink, and other stuff. (Sorry about the Biology 101 reference, but if you're reading a book called "Minibar Mixology" you could probably stand to inject a little erudition into your conversation.)

For most of its modern history, the minibar was pretty much just that: a miniature bar containing dozens of bottled drinks and mixers, which was all the liquid sustenance the jet-lagged, three-martini-lunch executives of the '70s and '80s really needed. In the last couple of decades, though, hotels discovered that men—and especially couples and families—do not live by beverages alone, and added snack items like peanuts and M&Ms (and occasionally, peanut M&Ms). These were quickly discovered to be a fast-growing profit center, since it's much easier for a five-year-old to sneak around dad's back and tear open a bag of pretzels than to successfully down two fingers of Dewar's.

More recently, the MBA types charged with wringing the maximum profit out of their hotels figured out that they could further increase revenue by packing their minibars with such items as hand towels, playing cards, condoms, massage oil, customized key chains, and Silly Putty. As a result, the average hotel minibar now looks like a drug store with hard liquor (and with much higher prices). Here's what you can expect to find:

DRINKS

✳ Single, airplane-size bottles of: vodka, gin, whiskey, rum, bourbon, and occasionally something fun (and even more expensive) like Midori or Cointreau

* Three or four cans of domestic or imported beer
  (Guess which ones cost more?)

* Five or six cans of cola and/or club soda

* Mixer-size cartons or bottles of orange juice, cranberry juice,
  iced tea, etc.

* A bottle of red, a bottle of white

* A teabag or two

* Enough bottled water to take a bath in

EATS

* Kindergarten-snack-size bags of: pretzels (salted and/or unsalted),
  potato chips (regular and sour cream and onion), M&M's,
  peanuts, pistachios, jelly beans, etc.

* All kinds of candy bars

* The occasional bagel

* The occasional fruit basket

OTHER STUFF

* Condoms (lubricated and unlubricated)

* Moist towelettes

* A corkscrew

* An extra bathrobe (This isn't really in the minibar, but at least you
  know how much it'll cost you if you take one home.)

* Disposable cameras

✳ An Etch-a-Sketch (Well, not really, but I wouldn't be surprised if some hotel, somewhere, had one.)

✳ Fat city, right? Your refrigerator at home is three times the size, and you couldn't fit half this stuff in. People go to school for years to learn how to stock a minibar—and when they're tired of that job, they arrange the seating on 747s.

THINGS YOU WON'T FIND IN YOUR MINIBAR

✳ Anything reasonably priced

✳ Food that would qualify as a meal (Hey, that's what room service is for.)

✳ A high-tech body fluid locator like they use on those undercover television specials

What You'll Find in Your Hotel Room

On the premise that most people don't really like to be away from home—and that folks who are forced to travel for a living like being away from home the least—the average hotel room sports more modern conveniences than a 40-year-old bachelor's efficiency apartment. Not everything a hotel provides will be germane to your minibar experience, but just for completeness' sake, it's helpful to take stock as soon as you check in (you'll be drunk later, so you might forget what you need) and special-order anything you think you might need, minibar-wise.

Here are some items that have become pretty much standard:

* A small, two-cup coffeemaker (For some reason, this is usually located in the bathroom.)

* A small, burrito-size microwave oven (bolted to the cabinet, of course)

* A small refrigerator with ice in the freezer (Which may or may not be separate from the minibar.)

* A whomping big TV equipped with basic cable

* A remote control for the whomping big TV, jammed under the sofa cushion

* An iron and ironing board

* A blender (You may want to request one if it's not provided; you'll need it.)

✳ A big mirror that makes you look fat

✳ A crappy little clock radio with an ear-piercing alarm

✳ High-speed Internet access (Sorry, you'll have to bring your own laptop.)

✳ A laptop (if you're staying at the kind of hotel Donald Trump stays at)

✳ Enough wooden hangers for the costume department of Radio City Music Hall

Since some of these items are essential for the recipes and party games scattered throughout this book, it's vitally important that you memorize them. I can't overemphasize this enough. Invite a friend over before your trip and have him drill you on them with flash cards. Recite them into a tape recorder and play them back when you're asleep. Tattoo them on your arm, if you must.

On second thought, you'll see them the minute you walk into your hotel room. Never mind. On to the fun!

A Brief Word about Expenses

By now, you're probably wondering what all this minibar madness is going to cost you. This is a perfectly reasonable question to ask. The fact is, even seasoned travelers are deeply terrified of their minibars, seeing them as inexhaustible pits of expense that can turn a simple $100 overnight stay into a $3,000 T&E-budget-busting extravaganza. To set your mind at ease, here's a representative list of minibar prices (remember to add the 8.25% sales tax, a 15% in-room service charge, and a 30% "Where else in this two-bit town do you think you're going to stay?" surcharge).

Looking at the minibar as you walk into your room $5

Thinking about using the minibar $7

Gingerly opening the minibar, then thinking better of it and

    slamming it shut again $10

Removing a single green M&M, crinkling the package

    shut, then stuffing it back into the minibar and hoping

    no one notices . . . . $30 and a call to your mom

Generic-brand potato chips $5

Fancy-brand potato chips $10

2.5-ounce bottle of no-name vodka $15

2.5-ounce bottle of a vodka you've actually heard of $25

See? Nothing to be worried about. (Although now may not be the best time to mention the latest trend in minibar technology: touch-sensor pads wired directly to the front desk of the hotel, alerting the staff when you've so much as breathed in the vicinity of a bag of pretzels.)

Seriously, though. Although raiding your minibar probably won't require you to take out a second mortgage, the 200 to 300% markup charged by most hotels can make Apu's Kwik-E-Mart on *The Simpsons* seem like a dollar store by comparison. We're talking $3 for a can of cola, $5 for a bag of pretzels, and $7 or $8 or $10 for a tiny, airplane-size bottle of Jack Daniels. Even a simple mixer like orange juice is likely to set you back three or four bucks, and we won't even get into the cost of calling room service at two in the morning and asking them (in a slurred voice, so you have to repeat yourself two or three times) to send up a bottle of almond bitters.

So what's a bone-weary traveler to do? The formula is complex, but it boils down to two main variables: your vacation budget on the one hand, and your expense account on the other.

TRAVELING FOR YOUR COMPANY

Let's get real: there is no corporation on the face of the earth that will reimburse an employee for a $75 banana daiquiri. Sensibly, the only folks who get compensated for such expenses are the ones who can most afford them, such as CEOs, senior VPs, and chairmen of the board—and if you belong in this select company, your room's minibar probably contains a foldout couch and a complimentary breakfast-in-bed, which puts you way beyond the purview of this book.

Even if you're just an ordinary middle-managing shlub, though, there are ways to make your corporate T&E department work for you. (I'm not saying there are ethical ways, but there are ways.) The key, of course, is how the minibar and other expenses are broken out on your hotel bill.

Imagine yourself slogging back to the office after three days in the Midwest, carrying two bills from two separate hotels. The first one looks like this:

Room rate $120

State tax $11.75

Incidental expenses $145

The second one looks like this:

Room rate $120

State tax $11.75

Out-of-room direct dial 900 number $15

Pay-per-View selection $10

One can Cheez-Wiz from minibar $7

Two bottles tequila from minibar @ $10/bottle $20

One carton orange juice from minibar $6

Three condoms from minibar @ $5 apiece $15

Room service, 8 oz. bottle of crème de coconut $45

Which bill do you think will be reimbursed in full? Sure, the T&E guy may ask what all those "incidental expenses" were about, but not for nothing were you promoted to tri-county sales manager of your boom-ing automotive company. You had to have your laundry done so you could look spiffy at that big meeting; you invited big clients up to your room for a drink; the two of you ordered room service because every restaurant in town closes at 8 PM. At worst, half of that $145 will be dis-allowed, meaning your company just treated you to the other half, a $70 room-service-and-minibar Bahama Mama (see page 150).

Sadly, the vast majority of hotels nowadays issue itemized bills of the second kind. Sure, this can put a bit of a damper on the average busi-ness trip, but looked at in a positive way, it can help you hone your sales-manship skills to executive-VP level. Remember all those episodes of *MacGyver* in which Richard Dean Anderson improvised homemade explosives from beach sand, lemon juice, and a breath mint? If you can convince your boss that you needed that crème de coconut to jimmy open the jammed lock on your room safe in which you stored crucial company documents, not only should he pay your bill in full, but you should be rewarded with a free, week-long vacation in Hawaii.

TRAVELING FOR YOURSELF

Quick, what's the key difference between traveling on behalf of your company and traveling for your own enjoyment? No, it's not the expense account (more about that below). It's that most business travel is perpetrated by weary, harassed, desperately lonely executive types, while it's much more likely that you'll be vacationing on your own dime with your children and/or significant other. This isn't to make some grand statement about the crushing burden inflicted by modern corporations on family life; it's simply to note that you're much more likely to crack that minibar if you're stranded in Des Moines on a rainy Tuesday, rather than partying it up with your wife on the Playa del Sol.

More than the lack of an expense account (and remember, your company probably won't reimburse you for those incidental expenses, anyway), it's the presence of other people that inhibits the average guy from whipping himself up a $50 minibar Mai-Tai (see page 158). Imagine the look on the face of your sad-eyed seven-year-old as it slowly dawns on him that daddy's impromptu cocktail means one day less at Disneyland. Even worse, imagine embarking on the four-hour drive home with your wife when she finds out the reason you wouldn't take her to that fancy French restaurant is that you loaded up that afternoon on $110 worth of minibar snack bags.

While it's true that not having a faceless corporation on which to foist your unreasonable expenses can make the hotel minibar a dicey proposition, remember that there's another type of faceless corporation on which people foist their unreasonable expenses all the time: credit-card companies. In the fullness of time, it won't matter to you whether that $900 hotel charge on your Visa bill covered five nights at the Marriott with your wife and kids, or two nights at the Marriot with your wife and kids and $600 worth of minibar and room-service charges. When it's mixed up with all the other stuff you charge on a regular basis (movies, bowling matches, figurines from all those shop-at-home television networks), it's easier just to pay what you can and get on with your life.

How to Deal with
Room Service

You can tell how experienced a hotel patron is by the way he or she orders from room service. The amateur traveler, no matter how unexceptional the circumstances—say, her flight was delayed a couple of hours, she's having a bad hair day, she's just plain too wiped out to make it down to the hotel restaurant—will still call room service in a small, trembling voice, as if she were about to ask to borrow money, and grossly overtip the delivery boy when he finally shows up. The world-class jet-setter, meanwhile, will blithely pick up the phone and order a whole roasted goat, and would you please slather that with dijon mustard, thank you.

The fact is, unless you're the type who carries a bottle of grenadine in his overnight bag, many of the drink recipes in this book will require the assistance of room service. There are two ways to deal with this unavoidable fact. One is to stick with those minibar concoctions, like the basic gin and tonic (page 61), that can be mastered in the privacy of your room, kind of like a shy thirteen-year-old playing in the corner with his chemistry set. The other is to embrace the concept of making room service work for you, The Customer, and not flinch from ordering whatever strange ingredients your palate demands and your budget will allow.

Working up the proper nerve aside, the main obstacle to ordering three overripe bananas, a dash of angostura bitters, and half a coconut from room service is the attitude of the hotel employee you're dealing with and the amount of detail you're willing to give. Consider the following exchange:

"Hi, I'd like to place an order, please."

"Yes, sir! How can I help you?"

"Well, this Breakfast Martini I've been whipping up (see page 36) isn't coming along exactly as I'd hoped. Mondays, right? Anyway, turns out it's not a real good idea to substitute pancake syrup for orange marmalade, so I was wondering if you could send a jar up. Of marmalade, I mean."

"Yes, I suppose we could..."

"And Cointreau. I forgot, the recipe needs Cointreau too. I was thinking of using another jigger of gin, but that wouldn't be much of a breakfast, would it? Send up a bottle of Cointreau."

"Sir, wouldn't it be easier just for you to..."

"And oh, yeah. Geez, I should have made a list, right? I'm having some people over later today, and I'm gonna need a few things. You got a pen and paper?"

Better would be something like this:

"Room service! How can I help you?"

"Please send a jar of orange marmalade and a bottle of Cointreau up to room 406." CLICK.

How to Deal with
Your Neighbors

There are two types of people who stay in hotels. The first type checks in early in the morning, throws her bags on the floor, goes out and does whatever she has to do, then returns late at night and collapses onto the bed exhausted. The second type doesn't have anything in particular planned, except for attending a couple of dull meetings or dinner parties and intends to avail himself of all the perks his hotel room has to offer. Since you're reading this book, odds are you belong in the second category.

Ideally, hotels would canvass patrons about their intentions, perhaps with a simple multiple-choice quiz distributed on check-in. Then, they could assign all Type 1 guests to the top few floors of the building, leave an empty floor or two in between, and stuff all the Type 2 guests into the few stories below that. Since very few hotels actually do this (in democratic countries, at least), there will occasionally be times when a hard-core Type 2 is assigned a room directly adjacent to a long-in-the-tooth Type 1.

That's where the trouble begins. Usually, a Type 1 has returned from a long day visiting Mom at the nursing home just as a Type 2 is getting his minibar party started. Depending how thick the walls of your hotel room are (and remember, thicker walls mean fewer rooms per floor), it's unlikely you'll be able to enjoy your midnight showing off the hotel's pay-an-arm-per-movie channel, complete with a fresh-made pitcher of Moscow Mules (see page 47) and travel-iron S'mores, without getting ratted on to the front desk or (worse) confronted in person by an enraged senior citizen.

Technically, of course, this is the hotel's problem, not yours. But in the interest of being an ethical guest, there are a few ways you can approach this situation:

* **Extend an invitation.** The key to this maneuver is determining how bedraggled and/or psychotic your neighbor is, and how he's likely to react to your unexpected largesse. If she needs convincing, show her a copy of this book and boast about your ability to whip up a citrus rum cooler (see page 37) in no time flat.

* **Stand your ground.** After a few minutes of pointless bickering, your neighbor will probably tromp down to the front desk and demand a new room away from you. The hotel may take care of this pesky neighbor for you!

* **Demand satisfaction.** Once the hotel manager gets involved, you have no chance of winning. Before you're transferred to another room or evicted out onto the street, insist that whatever you've taken out of your minibar be stricken from your bill. Since the odds of being complained about are directly proportional to the number of ingredients you've already used, this can save you a lot of money.

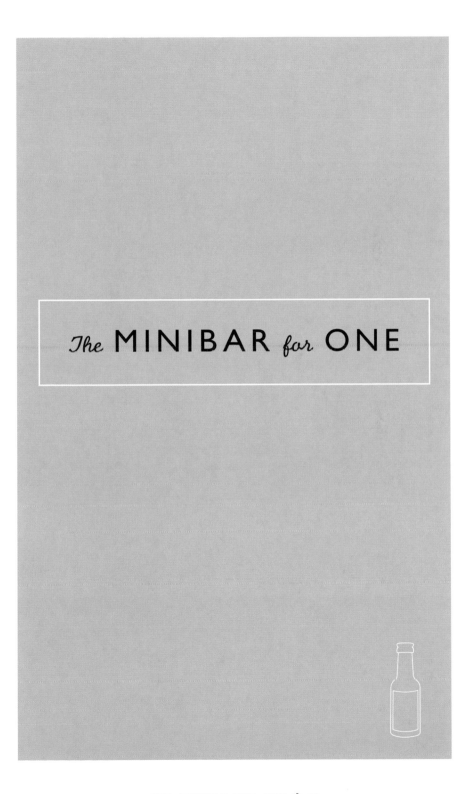

The MINIBAR for ONE

So your flight was delayed, they lost your luggage, it's raining outside, and you'd sooner change into your pajamas and order something on pay-per-view than ever leave your hotel room again for the rest of your life. You know what goes perfectly with a situation like this? Well, how about a minibar-vintage Bacardi Barracuda, or a homemade gin & tonic that actually contains a non-microscopic amount of gin for a change? As you peruse the following recipes, keep your trigger finger on the phone (you're going to have to order in some room service for special ingredients) and remember: you're The Customer, you deserve to have some fun!

Affinity

1 oz (30 ml) Scotch
$1/2$ oz (15 ml) dry vermouth
$1/2$ oz (15 ml) sweet vermouth
2 dashes orange bitters

Pour the ingredients into a mixing glass
with ice cubes. Stir well.
Strain into a chilled glass.

*

B&B

1 oz (30 ml) brandy
1 oz (30 ml) Bénédictine

Pour the brandy directly into a glass
and gently add the Bénédictine.

Affinity

Alexander

Alexander

1 oz (30 ml) cream

1 oz (30 ml) crème de cacao (brown)

1 oz (30 ml) brandy

Pour the ingredients into a shaker with ice cubes.
Shake well. Strain into a chilled cocktail glass.

＊

Trail Mix

Raisins

Dry cereal

Peanuts or other nuts

Granola

Candy pieces or chocolate chips

Mix any combination
of the above ingredients that
you like and enjoy.

Basic Fizz
4 oz (120 ml) club soda
2 oz (60 ml) desired liquor
1 oz (30 ml) lemon juice
1 teaspoon sugar

Pour the ingredients, including the club soda,
into a shaker over ice cubes. Shake well. Pour into a glass.
Foam will gather at the top.

✳

Basic Flip
2 oz (60 ml) desired liquor
$^3/_4$ oz (22 ml) cream
$^1/_2$ oz (15 ml) sugar syrup
1 egg yolk

Pour the ingredients into a shaker with ice cubes.
Shake vigorously. Strain into a chilled glass.
(If you can't pry an egg yolk out of room service,
you'll have to do without.)

Basic Pousse-Café

A minimum of 3 liquors and/or liqueurs
of varying densities and colors

Pour each ingredient slowly over the back
of a spoon into a glass. Begin with the heaviest liquor
and proceed to the lightest. The layers should
balance without blending.

Basic Sour

1^1/$_2$ oz (45 ml) desired liquor
1^1/$_2$ oz (45 ml) lemon juice
^{3}/$_4$ oz (22 ml) sugar syrup
maraschino cherry for garnish

Pour the ingredients into a shaker with ice cubes.
Shake well. Strain into a glass. Garnish with the cherry.
For a sour on the rocks, pour the ingredients into a glass,
stir well, add ice cubes, and garnish with the cherry.

Bolton Cocktail

1 ¾ oz (52 ml) vodka
⅓ oz (10 ml) peach schnapps
⅔ oz (20 ml) fresh raspberry purée
⅓ oz (10 ml) lemon juice
1 teaspoon liquid honey

Pour all ingredients into a shaker with ice.
Shake vigorously to dissolve the honey. Strain into a chilled glass.
Drop in a few raspberries, so when you're finished,
they'll be soaked with Bolton flavor.

Sal Calabrese says he created this cocktail for the American singer, Michael Bolton, who came into his bar and asked for something that *"matched his charming personality— and his expectations."* Don't try this yourself, unless you want room service to send up a carafe of Lestoil spiked with week-old capers.

Bolton Cocktail

Basic Frappé

2 oz (60 ml) desired liqueur

Fill a glass with shaved or crushed ice.
Pour in the liqueur.

✳

Basic Highball

2 oz (60 ml) desired liquor
water or club soda

Pour the liquor into a highball glass with ice cubes.
Fill with water or club soda.

Basic Rickie

lime wedge

5 oz (150 ml) club soda

2 oz (60 ml) desired liquor

Squeeze the lime juice from the wedge into
a highball glass with ice cubes. Drop the wedge into the glass.
Pour the remaining ingredients into the glass. Stir well.

Bacardi Barracuda

1^{1}/$_{2}$ oz (45 ml) Bacardi gold

^{2}/$_{3}$ oz (20 ml) Galliano

3^{1}/$_{2}$ oz (105 ml) pineapple juice

juice of one-half lime

Pour all ingredients into a shaker with ice.
Shake sharply. Strain into a glass filled with ice and
garnish with a wedge of lime.

Breakfast Martini

1³/₄ oz (52 ml) gin
¹/₂ oz (15 ml) Cointreau
juice of one-half lemon
1 teaspoon thin-sliced light orange marmalade

Place all ingredients into a shaker with ice.
Shake vigorously to enable the marmalade to combine well.
Strain into a chilled glass. Squeeze a thin twist of orange
on top (this gives it that extra bouquet of orange)
and garnish with a thin spiral of orange peel.

*Don't you wish you could be the kind of guy
who rolls out of his double-wide bed at 11 AM
on a work day, pours himself a bowl of Froot
Loops, and decamps in front of Good Morning
America with a pair of fuzzy slippers and a
drink as snazzy as this one? Be sure to pack
a swiss army knife for that thin-sliced
marmalade part, and whatever you do,
don't guzzle more than three of these before
that important lunch meeting.*

Chi Chi

1³/₄ oz (52 ml) vodka

1 oz (30 ml) coconut cream

4 oz (120 ml) pineapple juice

Pour all ingredients into a blender (assuming you
have one in your room, that is) with dry, crushed ice
and blend until smooth. Strain into a glass. Garnish with
a slice of pineapple and a maraschino cherry.

✱

Citrus Rum Cooler

1¹/₂ oz (45 ml) white rum

²/₃ oz (20 ml) triple sec or Cointreau

1³/₄ oz (52 ml) freshly squeezed orange juice

¹/₂ oz (15 ml) fresh lime juice

few dashes sugar syrup

Seven-Up

Pour ingredients into a shaker with ice.
Shake sharply. Strain into a glass filled with ice and fill
with Seven-Up. Garnish with a wedge of lime wrapped
in a spiral of orange peel that trails a little way
down the outside of the glass.

Game #1: Quarters

Granted, this frat-house favorite isn't quite as much fun when you're playing alone, but hard times call for hard measures. Ordinarily, players sit around a table with a mug of beer in the center, then to try to bounce a quarter off the surface and ker-plunk it into the brew—at which point, they can designate anyone they choose to drain the mug in a single gulp.

Since the image of a lonely traveler flipping quarters into $10 coffee cups of minibar beer is a bit, shall we say, pathetic, you might want to try the following variant. Stand as far away from the cup of beer as you possibly can, then fling, toss, or backhand any available change in its general direction. You don't have to plunk the quarter directly in; even a glancing blow is reason for celebration.

Not only does this version have the advantage of cutting down on your beer consumption, but think of all the exercise you'll get hurling quarters, then running over to find where they landed so you can do your laundry when you get back home.

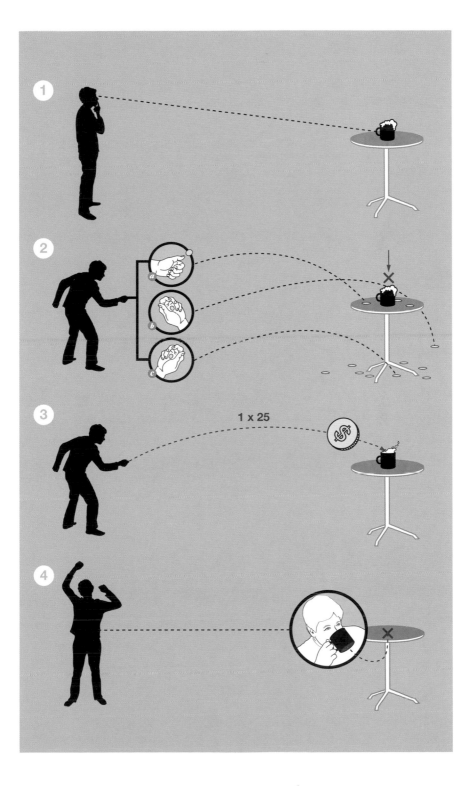

Cosmopolitan

Cosmopolitan

1³/₄ oz (52 ml) vodka

¹/₃ oz (10 ml) Cointreau

¹/₃ oz (10 ml) cranberry juice

¹/₃ oz (10 ml) fresh lime juice

Pour ingredients into a shaker with ice. Shake sharply.
Strain into a glass. Garnish with a wedge of lime.

*Here's one for all you lady travelers out there.
In all my life, I have never heard of a man
drinking a Cosmopolitan—and the fact is, if
the average guy was stuck in a hotel room in
a raging snowstorm with nothing but vodka,
Cointreau, and cranberry and lime juice, he'd
probably just shrug and pour himself some
tap water. Bottoms up!*

Dark and Stormy

1$^3/_4$ oz (52 ml) dark rum

juice of one-half lime

ginger beer

Pour the rum and lime juice into a glass filled
with ice and fill up with ginger beer.
Stir. Garnish with a twist of lime.

✳

El Diablo

1$^1/_2$ oz (45 ml) tequila

$^2/_3$ oz (20 ml) crème de cassis (black currant liqueur)

juice of one-half lime

ginger ale

Squeeze the lime juice into a glass half-filled
with crushed ice. Add the tequila and crème de cassis.
Fill up with ginger ale. Stir. Garnish with a fresh wedge
of lime dropped into the drink.

Garibaldi

1³/₄ oz (52 ml) Campari
3¹/₂ oz (105 ml) freshly squeezed orange juice

Pour the Campari, then the orange juice,
into a glass filled with ice. Stir.
Garnish with half a slice of orange.

Gin Rickey

1³/₄ oz (52 ml) gin
juice of 1 lime
soda water

Pour the gin and lime juice into a glass.
Top up with soda water and stir.
Garnish with a wedge of lime.

Hemingway Special

1³/₄ oz (52 ml) white rum
³/₄ oz (22 ml) grapefruit juice
¹/₃ oz (10 ml) maraschino liqueur
juice of one-half lime

Put all ingredients into a shaker with crushed ice.
Shake sharply. Strain into a chilled glass with fresh,
dry crushed ice and garnish with a wedge of lime.

Hemingway Hammer

²/₃ oz (20 ml) vodka
²/₃ oz (20 ml) white rum
¹/₃ oz (10 ml) blue curaçao
¹/₃ oz (10 ml) extra dry vermouth
¹/₃ oz (10 ml) freshly squeezed lime juice

Place all ingredients into a shaker with ice.
Shake quickly. Strain into a chilled glass.

Hemingway
Special

Hemingway
Hammer

Madras

1³/₄ oz (52 ml) vodka

4 oz (120 ml) cranberry juice

1 oz (30 ml) fresh orange juice

Pour each ingredient into a glass filled with ice.
Stir. Drop a wedge of lime into the glass.

✳

Monkey Shine

1 oz (30 ml) bourbon

1 oz (30 ml) banana liqueur

1 oz (30 ml) Bailey's Irish Cream

Pour all ingredients into a shaker with ice.
Shake. Strain into a chilled glass.

Mary Pickford

1½ oz (45 ml) white rum
1½ oz (45 ml) pineapple juice
6 drops of maraschino liqueur
1 teaspoon grenadine

Pour all ingredients into a shaker with ice.
Shake sharply. Strain into a chilled glass. Garnish with
a single maraschino cherry.

Moscow Mule

1¾ oz (52 ml) vodka
juice of one-half lime
ginger beer

Pour the vodka and lime juice into
the glass, then fill it up with ginger beer.
Garnish with a wedge of lime in the glass.

Martini

Martini

1 1/2 oz (45 ml) gin
1/2 teaspooon dry vermouth
1 green olive or lemon twist for garnish

Pour the ingredients into a mixing glass
with ice cubes. Stir well. Strain into a chilled martini glass.
Garnish with the olive or the lemon twist.

*

*This is one of those drinks I was always
fascinated by when I was a kid. Whenever
an adult in MAD magazine was shown
drinking, he was always drinking a martini,
and the three-martini lunch has been the
object of newspaper editorials and late-night
talk-show routines for the last 50 years.
So you can imagine how disappointed I
was when I finally snuck myself a fresh-made
martini and discovered that it was, er, an
"acquired taste." But hey, they're so popular,
somebody's got to like them, right?*

Game #2: The Reality TV Show Drinking Game

Raiding the minibar and watching junk TV go together like Bea Arthur and a *Golden Girls* reunion, so it's only natural to combine your two interests for a night of frolic and fun. Just switch on the tube, tune to any reality TV show (this shouldn't be hard, as there are something like seventeen airing on any given night), and take a big swig of your minibar concoction whenever a contestant:

* chokes down a cockroach.

* makes a frowny face to the camera behind her "ally's" back.

* suggests that "Alison," of all people, could certainly stand to eat a little bit less.

* wrings a weasel's neck with his bare hands.

* tans his bloated white stomach in the blazing tropical sun.

* demands to be switched to another hut.

* fringes his pants with a Bowie knife.

* pretends to be asleep while other people discuss her mental health.

* doesn't bother brushing the ants off her forearm.

* has a complete nervous breakdown.

* professes his undying love for a girl he just met.

Jamaican Mule

$3/4$ oz (52 ml) dark Jamaican rum
juice of one-half lime
ginger beer

Pour the rum and lime juice into the glass.
Top up with ginger beer. Garnish with a wedge
of lime in the glass.

Rossini

4 to 6 fresh strawberries
champagne
dry white wine

Put the strawberries in a blender, with a splash of wine,
and blend until smooth. Pour into a chilled glass and fill
up with champagne. Stir. Garnish with a strawberry.

Orange Pop

1$\frac{1}{2}$ oz (45 ml) vanilla vodka

orange soda

Pour the vodka into a glass with ice.
Top up with orange soda.

Scorpion

1 oz (30 ml) dark rum

$\frac{1}{2}$ oz (15 ml) white rum

$\frac{1}{2}$ oz (15 ml) brandy

$\frac{1}{3}$ oz (10 ml) triple sec or Cointreau

1$\frac{3}{4}$ oz (52 ml) freshly squeezed orange juice

juice of one-half lime

Pour all the ingredients into a shaker with ice.
Shake sharply. Strain into a glass filled with dry crushed ice.
Squeeze a wedge of lime directly in the drink
and then drop it in.

Grasshopper

³/₄ oz (22 ml) cream

³/₄ oz (22 ml) white crème de cacao

³/₄ oz (22 ml) green crème de menthe

Pour the ingredients into a shaker with ice cubes.
Shake well. Strain into a chilled glass.

*

Party Mix

Pretzels

Nuts

Cheese crackers

Mix packages of pretzels,
nuts, and crackers.
Variation: Add bagel chips
if available.

Grasshopper

Screwdriver
1³/₄ oz (52 ml) vodka
5 oz (150 ml) freshly squeezed orange juice

Pour the vodka into a glass. Add the orange juice and stir.
Garnish with a slice of orange.

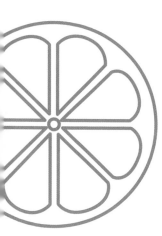

✳

Americano
1 oz (30 ml) Campari
1 oz (30 ml) sweet vermouth
club soda
lemon twist or orange slice for garnish

Fill a glass with ice cubes. Pour in the Campari
and the vermouth. Add the club soda. Garnish with
the lemon twist or orange slice.

Sunny Dream

2 tablespoons vanilla ice cream
$1\frac{1}{2}$ oz (45 ml) apricot brandy
$\frac{2}{3}$ oz (20 ml) Cointreau
$1\frac{3}{4}$ oz (52 ml) freshly squeezed orange juice
crushed ice

Put the ice cream into a blender and add the
remaining ingredients along with half a scoop of dry
crushed ice. Blend until smooth. Garnish with a
maraschino cherry and a sprig of mint.

*

Tequila Mockingbird

$1\frac{1}{2}$ oz (45 ml) silver tequila
$\frac{2}{3}$ oz (20 ml) green crème de menthe
juice of one-half lime

Pour all the ingredients into a glass filled with
crushed ice and fill up with soda water. Stir.
Garnish with a sprig of mint set in a wedge of lime
(if you can find either of them, that is).

Tropical Dawn

1 oz (30 ml) gin
$^2/_3$ oz (20 ml) Campari
$1^3/_4$ oz (52 ml) freshly squeezed orange juice

Place all the ingredients into a shaker with ice.
Shake sharply. Strain into a glass filled with crushed ice.
Garnish with a slice of orange and a cherry.

✳

Vampiro

$1^3/_4$ oz (52 ml) silver tequila
$2^1/_2$ oz (75 ml) tomato juice
1 oz (30 ml) orange juice
1 teaspoon clear honey
juice of half a lime
$^1/_2$ slice of onion, finely chopped
few thin slices of fresh red-hot chili
few drops of Worcestershire sauce
salt to taste

Pour all the ingredients into a shaker with ice.
Shake well to enable the flavor of the chili to be released
into the liquid. Strain into a glass filled with ice.
Garnish with a wedge of lime and a chili (green or red,
depending on your pain threshold).

Abbey Cocktail

$1^1/_4$ oz (37 ml) orange juice
$1^1/_4$ oz (37 ml) gin
2 dashes orange bitters

Pour the ingredients into a shaker with ice cubes.
Shake well. Strain into a chilled glass.
Garnish with a cherry.

✳

Dizzy

$1^1/_3$ oz (40 ml) bourbon
1 oz (30 ml) grappa
$^1/_2$ teaspoon liquid honey

Pour the bourbon, grappa, and honey into a shaker
with ice. Strain into a chilled glass.

Gin & Tonic

Gin & Tonic
2 oz (60 ml) gin

5 oz (150 ml) tonic water

Pour the ingredients into a glass with ice cubes.
Stir well. Garnish with a lime wedge.

*

You can always tell a bartender by the way he prepares a Gin & Tonic. Cheapskates hand you a big, cold, moisture-beaded glass that turns out to be 95% tonic water and 5% cheap gin, while good ol' Joe at the corner pub may skimp on the presentation, but give you a drink that's at least half brand-name alcohol. This is your chance to prepare your G&T the way you've always wanted it.

Whiskey Sour
1$^1/_2$ oz (45 ml) bourbon
1$^1/_2$ oz (45 ml) lemon juice
$^3/_4$ oz (22 ml) sugar syrup

Pour the ingredients into a shaker with ice cubes.
Shake well. Strain into a glass.
Garnish with a cherry.

✳

Chocolate Covered Pretzels
Chocolate bar or chips
Pretzels

Place chocolate bar in microwaveable
bowl and microwave on medium-high power
for 1 minute. Stir; microwave for additional
10-second intervals until melted.
Dip pretzels into melted chocolate
and set aside on plate to harden.

Whiskey Sour

Harvey Wallbanger

Harvey Wallbanger

$^3/_4$ oz (22 ml) vodka

1$^1/_2$ oz (45 ml) fresh orange juice

$^1/_4$ oz (7 ml) Galliano

Pour the vodka and orange juice into a glass
with ice cubes. Stir, then gently pour in the Galliano over
the back of a spoon. Garnish with a slice of orange
and a maraschino cherry.

✳

Ferrari

1 oz (30 ml) Amaretto

1$^3/_4$ oz (52 ml) dry vermouth

Pour the Amaretto into a glass with ice,
then add the vermouth. Stir.

Game #3: Fort

Have you seen the size of the comforter on a queen- or king-size hotel-room bed? Those things are big enough to shelter a refugee family of ten, and they're made of the kind of heavy, durable fabric that's usually used to protect the space shuttle during reentry. Clearly a piece of bedding of this Brobdingnagian size shouts one word in capital letters: FORT. (Unless you happen to be with your significant other, in which case it shouts an entirely different word that has only three letters.)

To make your fort, you'll need to jump onto the bed, puff the comforter over yourself like a giant marshmallow, and anchor it in place with four heavy objects (I suggest a travel iron, a Gideon's Bible, the top bureau drawer and the clock-radio, assuming you can remove it from its table.) Oh, yeah, I forgot to mention: place all your minibar equipment (bottles, mixers, glasses, etc.) onto the bed first, because once you're all warm and cozy inside you're not going to want to leave for any reason. Oh, and a flashlight, too—remember to bring a flashlight when you pack for your trip.

Angel's Delight

1$^1/_4$ oz (37 ml) cream
$^3/_4$ oz (22 ml) triple sec
$^3/_4$ oz (22 ml) gin
2–3 dashes grenadine

Pour the ingredients into a shaker with ice cubes.
Shake well. Strain into a chilled glass.

✳

Amber Cloud

1$^1/_3$ oz (40 ml) cognac
$^2/_3$ oz (20 ml) Galliano

Pour the ingredients into a shaker with ice.
Shake to create a cloud, then pour into a glass
filled with crushed ice.

Black Russian

1³/₄ oz (52 ml) vodka

³/₄ oz (22 ml) Kahlúa

Pour the ingredients into a glass with ice cubes.
Stir well.

Delilah

1¹/₂ oz (45 ml) gin

³/₄ oz (22 ml) Cointreau

³/₄ oz (22 ml) lemon juice

Pour the ingredients into a shaker with ice cubes.
Shake well. Strain into a chilled glass.

Dubonnet Cocktail

1 oz (30 ml) Dubonnet
$^3/_4$ oz (22 ml) gin

Pour the ingredients into a mixing glass with ice cubes.
Stir well. Strain into a chilled cocktail glass.
Garnish with a lemon twist.

✳

Gimlet

2 oz (60 ml) gin
$1^3/_4$ oz (52 ml) lime juice

Pour the ingredients into a mixing glass with ice cubes.
Stir well. Strain into a chilled glass.

A variety of gimlets can be made.
Simply substitute another primary liquor for the gin.
Rum, tequila, and vodka are good alternatives.

Gin & It
³/₄ oz (22 ml) sweet vermouth
1¹/₂ oz (45 ml) gin

Pour the vermouth directly into a glass without ice cubes.
Add the gin. Garnish with a cherry.

✳

Greyhound
2 oz (60 ml) vodka
4 oz (120 ml) grapefruit juice

Pour the ingredients into a glass with ice cubes.
Stir well.

Red Snapper

1 oz (30 ml) light rum
1 oz (30 ml) cream
$3/4$ oz (22 ml) Galliano
1 dash grenadine

Pour the ingredients into a shaker with ice cubes.
Shake well. Strain into a chilled glass.

*

Chocolate Covered Strawberries

Strawberries
Chocolate bar or chips

Order strawberries from room service or a nearby store. Place chocolate bar in microwaveable bowl and microwave on medium-high power for 1 minute. Stir; microwave for additional 10-second intervals until completely melted. Stir. Dip strawberries into melted chocolate and set aside on plate to harden.
Variation: Use banana in place of strawberry.

Red Snapper

Horse's Neck

spiral lemon peel
2 oz (60 ml) brandy
8 oz (240 ml) ginger ale
2–3 dashes Angostura bitters

Place the spiral lemon peel into a glass and secure
one end of the peel over the edge of the glass. Add ice cubes.
Pour the brandy and then the ginger ale. Add a dash
of bitters if you can find them. Stir well.

✱

Imperial

1 oz (30 ml) dry vermouth
1 oz (30 ml) gin
1 teaspoon maraschino liqueur

Pour the ingredients into a mixing glass with ice cubes.
Stir well. Strain into a chilled glass and garnish
with a lemon twist.

Irish Coffee

2 $\frac{1}{2}$ oz (75 ml) strong, hot coffee

1$\frac{1}{2}$ oz (45 ml) Irish whiskey

1 teaspoon brown sugar

1 oz (30 ml) whipping cream

Pour the first three ingredients into a hot drink mug.
Stir well. Float the cream on top.

Manhattan

1$\frac{1}{4}$ oz (37 ml) Canadian whiskey

$\frac{1}{2}$ oz (15 ml) sweet vermouth

2–3 dashes Angostura bitters

Pour the ingredients into a mixing glass with ice cubes.
Stir well. Strain into a chilled glass.
Garnish with a cherry.

Martinez

1 oz (30 ml) gin
$^3/_4$ oz (22 ml) dry vermouth
$^1/_4$ oz (7 ml) triple sec
1 dash orange bitters

Pour the ingredients into a mixing glass with ice cubes.
Stir well. Strain into a chilled glass. Twist a lemon
peel over the drink and drop it in.

Metropolitan

1$^1/_2$ oz (45 ml) brandy
1 oz (30 ml) sweet vermouth
$^1/_2$ teaspoon sugar syrup
2 dashes Angostura bitters

Pour the ingredients into a shaker with ice cubes.
Shake well. Strain into a chilled glass.

Monkey Hand

2 oz (60 ml) gin
1 oz (30 ml) orange juice
$1/4$ oz (7 ml) grenadine
1 dash Pernod

Pour the ingredients into a shaker with ice cubes.
Shake well. Strain into a chilled glass.
Garnish with an orange slice.

✳

Old Fashioned

1 sugar cube
2–3 dashes Angostura bitters
2 orange slices
2 oz (60 ml) bourbon
$1/2$ oz (15 ml) club soda

Place the sugar cube at the bottom of a glass
and saturate the cube with the bitters. Add one orange slice.
Muddle these ingredients. Fill the glass with ice cubes.
Add the bourbon and the club soda. Stir well. Garnish with
the second orange slice and a cherry.

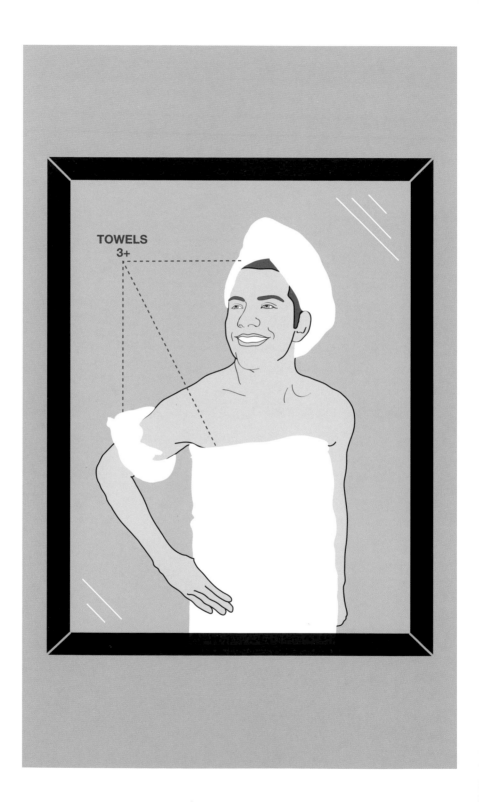

Game #4: The Queen of Sheba

If there's one thing hotels give you plenty of, free of charge, it's towels: full-size towels, mid-size towels, small towels, face and elbow towels, and seventeen different kinds of washcloths. It almost makes you wonder if they're expecting some kind of plumbing disaster, or if they are very concerned about your personal hygiene.

Anyway, The Queen of Sheba isn't a game, exactly, but it's fun to play in the same way a seven-year-old girl has fun dressing up in her mom's clothes and high heels. Simply wrap all the towels around yourself—the medium-size one around your head, the big one around your torso, the various hand towels and elbow towels and washcloths around your arms and legs—and announce to the mirror, "I'm the Queen of Sheba!" (If you're a guy, you may want to snap a digital picture of yourself to zap over to your frat buddies.)

Park Avenue

$1\frac{1}{2}$ oz (45 ml) gin

$\frac{1}{4}$ oz (7 ml) dry vermouth

$\frac{1}{4}$ oz (7 ml) sweet vermouth

$\frac{1}{4}$ oz (7 ml) unsweetened pineapple juice

Pour the ingredients into a mixing glass with ice cubes.
Stir well. Strain into a chilled glass.

✳

Rob Roy

$1\frac{1}{2}$ oz (45 ml) Scotch

1 oz (30 ml) sweet vermouth

1 dash Angostura bitters

Pour the ingredients into a mixing glass
with ice cubes. Stir well. Strain into a chilled glass.
Garnish with a cherry.

This drink can be perfected by using equal parts dry
and sweet vermouth.

Alaska

1³/₄ oz (52 ml) gin

²/₃ oz (20 ml) yellow Chartreuse

Stir the gin and chartreuse until they're completely mixed.
Strain into a chilled glass. (Some recipes recommend shaking
this drink, but this gives a cloudy effect.)

Dirty Mother

1¹/₃ oz (40 ml) brandy

1 oz (30 ml) Kahlúa

Pour the brandy into a glass with ice
and add the Kahlúa. Stir.

Rusty Nail
1$^{1}/_{2}$ oz (45 ml) Scotch
$^{3}/_{4}$ oz (22 ml) Drambuie

Pour the ingredients into a glass with ice cubes.
Stir well. Garnish with a lemon twist.

French Connection
1$^{3}/_{4}$ oz (52 ml) brandy
1 oz (30 ml) Amaretto

Fill a glass with ice, pour in the brandy
and Amaretto, stir and serve.

Rusty Nail

Barbara

1 oz (30 ml) vodka

1 oz (30 ml) white crème de cacao

1 oz (30 ml) cream

Pour all the ingredients into a shaker with ice cubes.
Strain into a chilled glass.
Garnish with a sprinkle of grated nutmeg.

✳

Sidecar

1^1/$_2$ oz (45 ml) cognac

^{3}/$_4$ oz (22 ml) Cointreau

^{1}/$_4$ oz (7 ml) lemon juice

Pour the ingredients into a shaker with ice cubes.
Shake well. Strain into a chilled glass.

Stinger

1³/₄ oz (52 ml) brandy
³/₄ oz (22 ml) white crème de menthe

Pour the ingredients into a glass with crushed ice.
Stir well. This drink can also be shaken over ice cubes
and strained into a chilled cocktail glass.

White Russian

1¹/₂ oz (45 ml) vodka
³/₄ oz (22 ml) Kahlúa
³/₄ oz (22 ml) cream

Pour the vodka and Kahlúa into a glass with ice cubes.
Stir. Gently top the drink with the cream.

Ward Eight

1³/₄ oz (52 ml) bourbon
¹/₂ oz (15 ml) lemon juice
¹/₂ oz (15 ml) orange juice
1 teaspoon grenadine

Pour the ingredients into a shaker with ice cubes.
Shake well. Strain into a chilled glass.
Garnish with a cherry.

Collins

juice of 1 lemon
1–2 dashes sugar syrup
1³/₄ oz (52 ml) gin
soda water

Add the lemon juice, sugar syrup, and gin to a glass.
Top up with soda. Stir. Garnish with a slice
of lemon dropped in the drink.

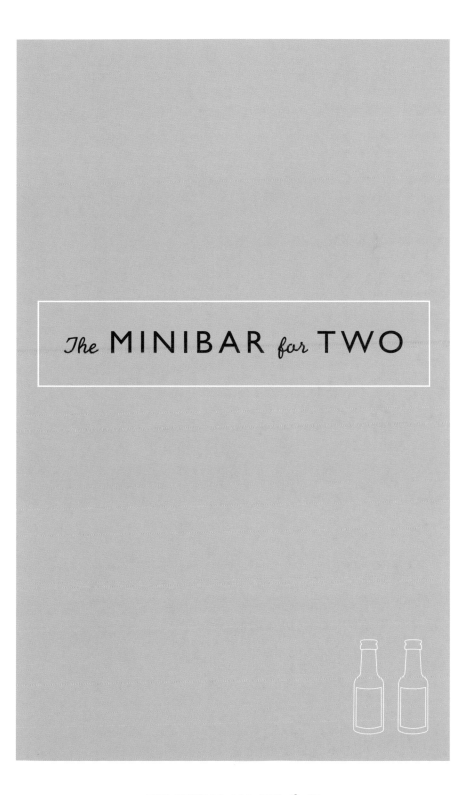

The MINIBAR for TWO

Not all the drinks concocted from your minibar need be enjoyed in the perfect, existential solitude of the traveling carpet salesman. If you're vacationing with your spouse or sweetheart—or if you just happen to be, um, "sharing a room" with that cute co-worker from the sales department—peruse the following pages for recipes that'll light a love-combusting fire under that king-size bed you specified when you made your reservations. And if all your best-laid plans come to naught, well, with tasty treats like a fresh-made Love in the Afternoon or Sex on the Beach, at least the entire evening won't have gone to waste.

Añejo Highball
1¹/₂ oz (45 ml) añejo rum
¹/₂ oz (15 ml) orange curaçao
¹/₂ oz (15 ml) freshly squeezed lime juice
2 dashes Angostura bitters
4 oz (120 ml) ginger beer

Fill a glass with ice cubes. Pour the spirits in first,
then the lime juice, bitters, and ginger beer and stir.
Garnish with a slice of lime and orange.

＊

Bay Breeze
1¹/₂ oz (45 ml) vodka
²/₃ oz (20 ml) peach schnapps
3¹/₂ oz (105 ml) cranberry juice
1³/₄ oz (52 ml) pineapple juice

Pour all ingredients into a shaker with ice.
Shake sharply. Strain into a glass filled with ice and garnish
with a wedge of lime.

Bay of Passion

1 oz (30 ml) vodka

1 oz (30 ml) Passoã liqueur

1$\frac{1}{2}$ oz (45 ml) pineapple juice

2$\frac{3}{4}$ oz (82 ml) cranberry juice

Pour all the ingredients into a shaker with ice.
Shake sharply. Strain into a glass with ice. Garnish with
a thin slice of orange and a maraschino cherry.

Blue Heaven

1 oz (30 ml) Bacardi white rum

$\frac{1}{2}$ oz (15 ml) Amaretto

$\frac{1}{2}$ oz (15 ml) blue curaçao

$\frac{1}{2}$ oz (15 ml) fresh lime juice

3$\frac{1}{2}$ oz (105 ml) pineapple juice

Pour all the ingredients into a shaker with ice.
Shake sharply. Strain into a highball glass filled with ice.
To garnish, place a maraschino cherry, a wedge
of pineapple, and a small pineapple leaf on a cocktail
stick and place it on the rim.

Bella Taormina

1 oz (30 ml) gin
$^2/_3$ oz (20 ml) Aperol
$^1/_2$ oz (15 ml) limoncello
$^1/_2$ oz (15 ml) mandarin liqueur
$^2/_3$ oz (20 ml) freshly squeezed orange juice

Pour all ingredients into a shaker with ice.
Shake sharply. Strain into a chilled glass. Garnish with
a kumquat (if you can get room service to procure one)
cut like a flower, and a spiral of lime.

When you call room service for this one,
you may have to explain what "Aperol" is—
it sounds like the kind of mouthwash they sell
at the drugstore, but it's actually an orange
liqueur from Italy. Granted, in the context of
the other things you'll need to have sent up—
like the limoncello and mandarin liqueur,
not to mention that pesky kumquat—room
service will probably be hip to the fact that
Aperol is some kind of drink. If not, at least
you and your sweetheart will be minty-fresh
the next morning.

Bella Taormina

Blue Lagoon

1 oz (30 ml) blue curaçao
1 oz (30 ml) vodka
Seven-Up

Pour the blue curaçao and the vodka into a glass.
Top up with Seven-Up. Garnish with a maraschino
cherry and a slice of lemon.

Caribbean Breeze

$1^{1}/_{2}$ oz (45 ml) dark rum
$^{1}/_{3}$ oz (10 ml) banana liqueur
$2^{1}/_{2}$ oz (75 ml) pineapple juice
$1^{3}/_{4}$ oz (52 ml) cranberry juice
$^{1}/_{3}$ oz (10 ml) Rose's lime cordial

Pour all the ingredients into a shaker filled with ice.
Shake. Strain into a glass with crushed ice.
Garnish with a slice of lime.

Cool Breeze

1 oz (30 ml) Midori (melon liqueur)
1 oz (30 ml) gold tequila
1 oz (30 ml) cranberry juice

Pour all the ingredients into a shaker with ice.
Shake sharply. Strain into a glass.
Garnish with a wedge of lime.

Dream Cocktail

1 oz (30 ml) Dubonnet
$\frac{1}{2}$ oz (15 ml) Cointreau
$\frac{1}{2}$ oz (15 ml) grapefruit juice
champagne

Pour each ingredient, except the champagne,
into the mixing glass filled with ice. Stir. Pour into a chilled
glass and fill it up with champagne. Stir again.
Garnish with a quarter of a pink grapefruit slice.

Elise
1½ oz (45 ml) gin
½ oz (15 ml) limoncello
½ oz (15 ml) peach schnapps
2½ oz (75 ml) grapefruit juice
2½ oz (75 ml) mango juice
⅓ oz (10 ml) Orgeat (almond syrup)

Pour all the ingredients into a shaker with ice.
Shake sharply. Strain into a glass. Garnish with a cape
gooseberry (available at all finer hotels).

Hurricane Cooler
1½ oz (45 ml) dark rum
⅔ oz (20 ml) white rum
⅔ oz (20 ml) fresh lime juice
1¾ oz (52 ml) passionfruit juice
1 oz (30 ml) pineapple juice
1 oz (30 ml) freshly squeezed orange juice
⅓ oz (10 ml) black currant syrup

Pour all the ingredients into a shaker with ice.
Shake sharply. Strain into a glass filled with crushed ice.
Garnish with a slice of pineapple and a cherry.

Imagination

1 passionfruit
1$\frac{1}{2}$ oz (45 ml) vodka
1$\frac{1}{2}$ oz (45 ml) clear apple juice
ginger ale

Cut the passionfruit in half and scoop out the flesh.
Put it in the shaker with dry, crushed ice and add the vodka
and apple juice. Shake sharply. Pour into a chilled glass.
Fill up with ginger ale and stir.

Long Island Iced Tea

$\frac{1}{3}$ oz (10 ml) white rum
$\frac{1}{3}$ oz (10 ml) gin
$\frac{1}{3}$ oz (10 ml) vodka
$\frac{1}{3}$ oz (10 ml) tequila
$\frac{1}{3}$ oz (10 ml) Cointreau
juice of 1 lime
chilled Coca-Cola

Pour all the ingredients, except the cola, into a glass.
Stir. Top up with chilled cola and garnish
with a wedge of lime.

Piña Colada

Love
in the
Afternoon

Piña Colada

3½ oz (105 ml) pineapple juice, or three slices canned pineapple
1¾ oz (52 ml) coconut cream
1¾ oz (52 ml) white rum
crushed ice

Pour the pineapple juice into a blender and add
the coconut cream and white rum. Blend for a few seconds.
Add the crushed ice and blend for five seconds.
Pour into a glass. Garnish with a quarter slice
of fresh pineapple speared with a maraschino
cherry, or put a star fruit on the rim.

Love in the Afternoon

5 strawberries
1 oz (30 ml) dark rum
1 oz (30 ml) fresh orange juice
1 oz (30 ml) coconut cream
½ oz (15 ml) strawberry liqueur
½ oz (15 ml) fresh cream
crushed ice

Place the strawberries in a blender and add the liquids.
Add a scoop of dry, crushed ice. Blend for 10 to 15 seconds until
smooth. Pour into a glass. Garnish with a strawberry
with a mint leaf inserted in its top.

Melon Ball

1 oz (30 ml) vodka
²/₃ oz (20 ml) Midori (melon liqueur)
3¹/₂ oz (105 ml) pineapple juice

Pour all the ingredients into a shaker with ice.
Shake well. Strain into a glass filled with ice. Garnish with
a couple of tiny balls of melon, in different colors if possible,
speared on a toothpick on the edge of the glass.

✳

Monza

²/₃ oz (20 ml) vodka
²/₃ oz (20 ml) crème de cassis (black currant liqueur)
2²/₃ oz (80 ml) grapefruit juice

Pour all the ingredients directly into a glass filled with dry,
crushed ice. Stir to bring out the deep purple color.

Perini

1³/₄ oz (25 ml) fresh pear purée
1³/₄ oz (25 ml) cranberry juice
¹/₃ oz (10 ml) pear schnapps
champagne

To make the pear pureé, peel a ripe pear and remove the core.
Put it in a blender with a dash of dry white wine
and blend until smooth. Add equal quantities of cranberry juice
and pear pureé to the glass. Add a dash of schnapps and fill
with champagne. Stir. Garnish with a slice of pear
and a few cranberries on a stem.

✳

Sex on the Beach

1 oz (30 ml) vodka
¹/₂ oz (15 ml) peach schnapps
¹/₂ oz (15 ml) Chambord (black raspberry liqueur)
1³/₄ oz (52 ml) freshly squeezed orange juice
1³/₄ oz (52 ml) cranberry juice

Pour all the ingredients in a shaker with ice.
Shake sharply. Strain into a glass filled with ice.
Garnish with a slice of lime.

Game #5: Condom Balloon Animals

If you're in the kind of hotel that puts expensive condoms in its minibar, here's your chance both to entertain yourself and to impress that cutie at the front desk. As any tenth-grader can tell you, condoms can be blown up into cute hot-doggy shapes, just like clown balloons. If your minibar has only two or three on hand, you'll have to content yourself with an inflatable pretzel, but a pack of a dozen or more can be used to make a quite impressive giraffe.

Okay, that's the fun part. So how do you impress that check-in clerk? Simple: If you're staying for more than one night, the Minibar Police will already have noted that you've used every single condom in your hotel room. Since hotel work tends to be extremely dull, this licentious snippet of information will make the rounds of the staff post-haste, meaning the next time you make your way downstairs, the entire staff will know about your illicit activities.

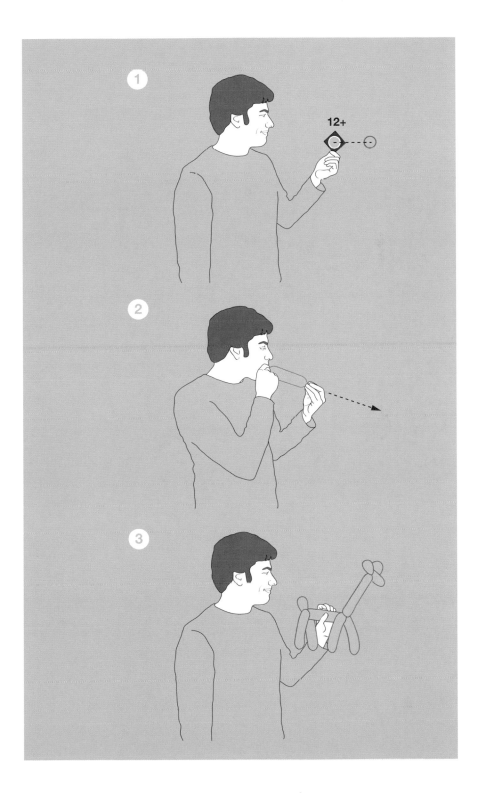

Miami Spice

Miami Spice
1 1/2 oz (45 ml) spiced rum
2/3 oz (20 ml) Cointreau
1 1/2 oz (45 ml) orange juice
1 1/2 oz (45 ml) papaya juice
2/3 oz (20 ml) lime juice

Place all the ingredients into a shaker with ice.
Shake sharply. Strain into a glass filled with ice. Garnish with
an orange slice, a slice of lime, and a maraschino cherry
in the middle, all speared on a toothpick across the glass.

*

Covered Banana
Banana
Yogurt or honey
Granola

Peel banana and cut in half.
Dip into yogurt or honey and roll
in granola until the banana
is covered.

Silver Sunset

1 oz (30 ml) vodka
$^1/_2$ oz (15 ml) apricot brandy
$^1/_2$ oz (15 ml) Campari
3 oz (90 ml) fresh orange juice
$^1/_2$ oz (15 ml) lemon juice
1 dash egg white

Pour all the ingredients into a shaker with ice.
Shake sharply. Strain into a glass filled with ice. Garnish with
a slice of orange and a maraschino cherry.

✳

Lady Love

1 oz (30 ml) curaçao
1 oz (30 ml) ruby port
$^1/_2$ oz (15 ml) white crème de menthe
$^1/_2$ oz (15 ml) crème de mûre (blackberry liqueur)

Pour all the ingredients into a shaker with ice.
Shake. Strain into a chilled glass.

Summer Love
1 oz (30 ml) citron vodka
$\frac{1}{2}$ oz (15 ml) Pisang Ambon liqueur
$\frac{1}{2}$ oz (15 ml) limoncello
juice of one-half lemon
bitter lemon

Place the vodka, Pisang, limoncello, and lemon juice into
a shaker with ice. Shake sharply. Strain into a glass filled with ice.
Top up with bitter lemon. Garnish with a star fruit.

Pisang Ambon is a delicious green liqueur based
on an old Indonesian recipe of exotic herbs and fruits.
(Which is to say, you may or may not be able to
get it from room service.)

✳

Sweetheart
1 oz (30 ml) vodka
$1\frac{1}{2}$ oz (45 ml) Aperol
$\frac{2}{3}$ oz (20 ml) limoncello
$\frac{2}{3}$ oz (20 ml) freshly squeezed lemon juice
$3\frac{1}{2}$ oz (105 ml) cranberry juice

Put all the ingredients into a shaker with ice.
Shake quickly. Strain into a glass filled with ice. Garnish with
a stem of cranberries on the rim of the glass.

John Daniels

1½ oz (45 ml) Jack Daniels

⅔ oz (20 ml) Amaretto

⅓ oz (10 ml) freshly squeezed lemon juice

ginger ale

Put the Jack Daniels, Amaretto, and lemon juice into
a shaker with ice. Shake. Strain into a glass with ice and fill
up with ginger ale. Garnish with a thin slice
of orange dropped in the drink.

Slow-Hand Lover

1 oz (30 ml) tequila

⅔ oz (20 ml) dark rum

⅓ oz (10 ml) Tia Maria

⅔ oz (20 ml) coconut cream

one-half fresh banana

⅓ oz (10 ml) pineapple juice

Pour all the ingredients, except the rum, into a blender
with a scoop of crushed ice. Blend for 15 seconds. Pour into a chilled
glass. Float the rum on top. Garnish with a cape gooseberry.

John Daniels

Slow-Hand Lover

Mint Julep

bunch of fresh mint leaves
1 teaspoon superfine sugar
1³/₄ oz (52 ml) bourbon
1 tablespoon cold water

Place the mint in the glass. Add the sugar and water.
Crush the mint with the back of a spoon until the sugar dissolves
and the fragrance of the mint is released. Add the bourbon.
Fill the glass with dry, crushed ice and stir.
Garnish with a sprig of mint.

✳

The drink's name is (supposedly) derived
from the ancient Arabic word "julab,"
meaning "rose water." By the fourteenth
century, "julep" became the word for a
syrup of sugar and water, which was mainly
used as a solvent for medicine. How the
rose-water "julab" turned into the minty
"julep" is a subject for experts in antebellum
Southern history, which I am decidedly not.

Mint Julep

Pimm's

Pimm's

2 oz (60 ml) Pimm's No. 1

3 oz (90 ml) Seven-Up or lemon-lime soda

Pour the Pimm's into a glass filled with ice.
Top up with Seven-Up. Garnish with a slice of lemon
peel or slice and a cucumber peel or slice.

*

This drink was created in 1840 as a digestive
tonic (kind of an early form of Alka-Seltzer)
by James Pimm, who ran an oyster bar in
London's financial center. Like Coca-Cola,
Pimm's No. 1 has a secret recipe, and lives
in legend as the only premixed cocktail used
by professional bartenders. In other words:
no, you're not gonna find this one in your
minibar, and when you call room service,
you'll have to give them the secret password
to get them to cooperate.

Game #6: Obstacle Course

There are two possible explanations for why hotels cram so much useless furniture—bureaus, sofas, armchairs, writing desks, etc.—into their rooms. One is that they expect guests to move in permanently and not notice that they're spending $15,000 a month when they could rent an apartment in the nice part of town for one-tenth that amount. The other is that the hotel is encouraging its patrons to indulge in a little minibar-fueled feng shui, and rearrange their carefully appointed suites to replicate a marine obstacle course.

Needless to say, I lean toward the latter interpretation. Since boot-camp training isn't to everyone's taste, beginners may simply want to arrange their furniture in a zig-zag pattern, shout "Serpentine!," and duck and weave as if they're avoiding enemy gunfire.

If you consider yourself an advanced guest, try clearing a path in front of the bed, then down a couple of minibar Mai Tais and test your hurdling skills (or simply land gracefully on the bed—it's fun either way). If the guest directly below you complains about the noise, tell the front desk you were looking for a lost contact lens.

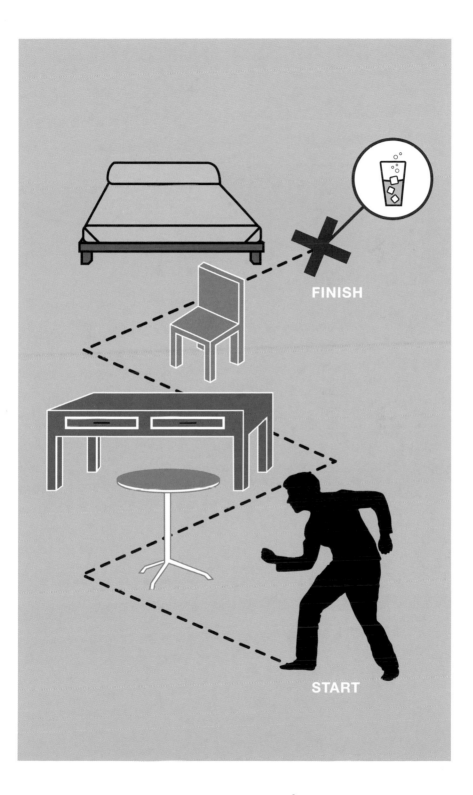

FINISH

START

Happy World
$^1/_2$ oz (15 ml) brandy
1 oz (30 ml) Cointreau
1 oz (30 ml) orange juice
$^1/_2$ oz (15 ml) banana liqueur

Pour the brandy and Cointreau, then the juice and banana liqueur, into a shaker with ice. Shake and strain into a glass.

*

Woo-Woo
1 oz (30 ml) vodka
$^2/_3$ oz (20 ml) peach schnapps
$1^3/_4$ oz (52 ml) cranberry juice

Pour all the ingredients into a shaker with ice.
Shake sharply. Strain into a glass filled with ice. Garnish with a wedge of lime dropped in the drink.

Adonis

1 oz (30 ml) dry sherry
$\frac{1}{2}$ oz (15 ml) sweet vermouth
$\frac{1}{2}$ oz (15 ml) dry vermouth
2 dashes orange bitters

Pour the ingredients into a mixing glass with ice cubes.
Stir well. Strain into a chilled glass.

Bellini

Fresh white peach purée
champagne

Quarter-fill a chilled glass with peach purée
and fill up with the champagne. Stir.
Garnish with a slice of peach on the rim.

Maiori Magic

Velvet Rosa

Maiori Magic

1 1/2 oz (45 ml) Campari
2/3 oz (20 ml) limoncello
2/3 oz (20 ml) lemon juice
tonic water

Pour the Campari directly into a glass filled with ice.
Add the limoncello and lemon juice. Fill up with tonic.
Stir, squeeze a wedge of lime on top and drop
it into the drink.

Velvet Rosa

2/3 oz (20 ml) white rum
1/3 oz (10 ml) peach schnapps
1 oz (30 ml) cranberry juice
champagne

Put all the ingredients, except the champagne,
into a shaker with ice. Shake quickly. Strain into a chilled glass
and fill up with champagne. Stir quickly to bring the
effervescence into play. Garnish with a small, delicate red rose
petal (maybe there'll be one out in the hotel garden).

Between the Sheets
$^3/_4$ oz (22 ml) brandy
$^3/_4$ oz (22 ml) light rum
$^3/_4$ oz (22 ml) triple sec
$^1/_2$ oz (15 ml) lemon juice

Pour the ingredients into a shaker with ice cubes.
Shake well. Strain into a chilled glass.
Garnish with a lemon twist.

Campari Cocktail
1 oz (30 ml) Campari
$^3/_4$ oz (22 ml) vodka
1 dash Angostura bitters

Pour the ingredients into a shaker with ice cubes.
Shake well. Strain into a chilled glass.
Garnish with a lemon twist.

Nightcap Cocktail

1 oz (30 ml) anisette

1 oz (30 ml) curaçao

1 oz (30 ml) brandy

1 egg yolk

Pour all the ingredients into a shaker with ice.
(And pack an egg in your luggage—room service may
find your request a bit strange.)

✳

Fuzzy Navel

3 oz (90 ml) orange juice

1 oz (30 ml) vodka

1 oz (30 ml) peach liqueur

Pour the ingredients into a glass with ice cubes.
Stir well.

Champagne Cocktail

1 sugar cube
2–3 dashes Angostura bitters
champagne
1 oz (30 ml) brandy

Place the sugar cube in the bottom of a glass.
Saturate the cube with the Angostura bitters.
Pour in the champagne. Add the brandy.
Garnish with an orange slice and maraschino cherry.

As you can see, this drink requires a lot of preparation, but on the plus side, it's the only recipe in this book (besides the Breakfast Martini) that can plausibly be assembled before noon. In fact, while your companion is asleep, you may want to add a generous brunch order to your request for Angostura bitters. There's nothing better than waking up to a pitcher of champagne cocktails and a heaping stack of pancakes.

Champagne Cocktail

Golden Cadillac

3/4 oz (22 ml) cream

3/4 oz (22 ml) white crème de cacao

3/4 oz (22 ml) Galliano

Pour the ingredients into a shaker with ice cubes.
Shake well. Strain into a chilled glass.

Golden Dawn

3/4 oz (22 ml) gin

3/4 oz (22 ml) apricot brandy

3/4 oz (22 ml) calvados

3/4 oz (22 ml) orange juice

Pour the ingredients into a shaker with ice cubes.
Shake well. Strain into a chilled glass.

Golden Dream

$^3/_4$ oz (22 ml) cream
$^3/_4$ oz (22 ml) orange juice
$^3/_4$ oz (22 ml) Cointreau
$^3/_4$ oz (22 ml) Galliano

Pour the ingredients into a shaker with ice cubes.
Shake well. Strain into a chilled glass.

Melon Patch

1 oz (30 ml) melon liqueur
$^1/_2$ oz (15 ml) triple sec
$^1/_2$ oz (15 ml) vodka
4 oz (120 ml) club soda

Pour the first three ingredients into a shaker
with ice cubes. Shake well. Strain into a
glass with ice cubes. Add the club soda.
Garnish with an orange slice.

Game #7:
Gideon Bible Word Search

The suite you paid so much for may not have a working TV, and it's a 50-50 proposition whether you'll even find a bed in there. But the one thing you can be absolutely sure to locate in your hotel room is a brand-spanking-new Gideon Bible. And since the Gideons went through so much trouble (presumably) to put it there, it would be churlish of you not to amuse yourself with it. (Those of a more God-fearing disposition can skip this page and proceed directly to Toilet Paper Tug-of-War on page 157.)

The trick to enjoying your Gideon Bible is not actually to read it, but to emulate the author of *The Bible Code* and scour it for hidden messages. This can be done by:

 writing down the fourteenth (or twenty-seventh, or fifty-sixth) word on every other page, then arranging the results into a coherent sentence.

 opening the bible at random and memorizing the verse that most closely matches the score of last week's Giants-Raiders game.

 manipulating the Aramaic cognates of old Hebraic passive verbs for hints to the pending apocalypse.

Hot Toddy

1 1/2 oz (45 ml) blended whiskey
1/2 oz (15 ml) lemon juice
1/2 oz (15 ml) honey
1/4 oz (7 ml) sugar syrup
hot water

Pour the first four ingredients into a hot drink mug.
Stir well. Fill the mug with hot water. Stir again.
Garnish with a lemon slice spiked with cloves,
and a cinnamon stick, if you can find them.

Nutty Professor

1 oz (30 ml) Grand Marnier
1 oz (30 ml) Frangelica
1 oz (30 ml) Bailey's Irish Cream

Pour all the ingredients into a shaker with ice.
Shake and strain into a glass.

Hot Toddy

Kir

Kir

$^1/_4$ oz (7 ml) crème de cassis
2 $^1/_4$ oz (67 ml) dry white wine

Pour the crème de cassis into a wine glass.
Slowly add the dry white wine. To make a Kir Royale,
substitute champagne for the dry white wine.

Hot Kiss

1 oz (30 ml) Irish whiskey
$^1/_2$ oz (15 ml) white crème de menthe
$^1/_2$ oz (15 ml) white crème de cacao
4 oz (120 ml) hot coffee
$^2/_3$ oz (20 ml) fresh cream

Pour the liqueurs and whiskey into a mug.
Add the coffee and cream and stir. Serve hot.

Negroni

$^3/_4$ oz (22 ml) sweet vermouth
$^3/_4$ oz (22 ml) Campari
$^3/_4$ oz (22 ml) gin

Pour the ingredients into a glass with ice cubes. Stir well.
Garnish with an orange slice.

✳

Louisville Lady

1 oz (30 ml) bourbon
$^1/_2$ oz (15 ml) white crème de cacao
$^1/_2$ oz (15 ml) fresh cream

Pour the bourbon and crème de cacao into
a shaker with ice. Shake well. Strain into a glass
and gently float the fresh cream on top.

Negroni

Sea Breeze

Sea Breeze

1³/₄ oz (53 ml) vodka

3 oz (90 ml) cranberry juice

1 oz (30 ml) grapefruit juice

Pour the vodka and cranberry juice into a glass
with ice cubes. Stir well. Top the drink with the grapefruit
juice. Garnish with a grapefruit slice.

White Lady

1¹/₂ oz (45 ml) gin

³/₄ oz (22 ml) Cointreau

³/₄ oz (22 ml) lemon juice

Pour all the ingredients into a shaker with ice,
shake, and strain into a chilled glass.

Yellow Bird

juice of one-half lime

1$^{1}/_{4}$ oz (37 ml) orange juice

1 oz (30 ml) light rum

1 oz (30 ml) dark rum

$^{1}/_{4}$ oz (7 ml) Galliano

Squeeze the lime juice into a shaker with ice.
Add all the remaining ingredients. Shake well.
Strain into a glass with crushed ice.
Garnish with a cherry.

Yogurt Cups

Yogurt

Fresh fruit

Walnuts or peanuts

Granola

Chop fruit into small pieces.
Place yogurt into bowl
and top with chopped fruit,
nuts, and granola.

Yellow Bird

French 75

French 75
$^1/_4$ oz (7 ml) lemon juice
$^1/_4$ oz (7 ml) gin
$^1/_4$ oz (7 ml) Cointreau
5 oz (150 ml) champagne

Pour the lemon juice, gin, and Cointreau into a shaker with ice cubes. Shake well. Strain into a chilled glass. Carefully add the champagne.

✳

If you prefer, vodka can be substituted for gin; that cocktail is called a French 76. I'm not sure what constitutes a French 77, 78, and so forth, but if you and your honey are bored, feel free to experiment with whatever liquors happen to be on hand. It's very unlikely that anything you choose will spontaneously combust in the presence of lemon juice and cointreau, but just in case, step well back from the glass before you start your experiment.

Lemon Drop

1½ oz (45 ml) vodka

¾ oz (22 ml) lemon juice

1 teaspoon sugar syrup

Pour the ingredients into a shaker with ice cubes.
Shake well. Strain into a chilled glass
and garnish with a lemon twist.

Diana Cocktail

1¾ oz (52 ml) white crème de menthe

⅔ oz (20 ml) brandy

Fill a glass with finely crushed ice
and pour in the crème de menthe.
Gently float the brandy on top.

Lemon Drop

Pink Lady

Pink Lady

1$\frac{1}{2}$ oz (45 ml) gin

$\frac{1}{4}$ oz (7 ml) lemon juice

1–2 dashes grenadine

1 egg white

Pour the ingredients into a shaker with ice cubes.
Shake well and strain into a chilled glass.
Garnish with a cherry.

Ice Cream Sundae

Bowl of ice cream
Individual package of cookies

Order ice cream in your favorite
flavor from room service or a nearby ice
cream shop. Using a cup, crush the
unopened package of cookies.
Sprinkle the cookie crumbs on
top of the ice cream.

Sazerac
1 sugar cube
1 dash Peychaud bitters
2 oz (60 ml) rye whiskey
½ teaspoon Pernod
water or club soda

Place the sugar cube at the bottom of a glass.
Saturate the cube with a dash of bitters. Muddle.
Add the whiskey and the Pernod. Mix well.
Fill the glass with the water or club soda.
This drink is always served neat.

Oh, My Gosh
1 oz (30 ml) Amaretto
1 oz (30 ml) peach schnapps

Pour both ingredients into a glass
with ice and stir.

The MINIBAR PARTY

Okay, picture the following situation: Desperate to secure that new contract that'll mean the difference between Chapter 7 bankruptcy and a thriving fiscal year, your CEO has dispatched the entire seventeenth floor of your office building to the annual convention in Salt Lake City. Since there are only so many events that one can organize, you and your co-workers find yourself with lots of down time on your hands and the combined power of 38 minibars at your disposal. What choice do you have but to put your budgets together and party on down with the recipes in this chapter? (Note: You'll have to scale up the ingredients according to the number of revelers—get the accountant in your bunch to do the math.)

Bloody Mary

Bloody Mary

5 oz (150 ml) tomato juice
^{2}/$_3$ oz (20 ml) fresh lemon juice
1^3/$_4$ oz (52 ml) vodka
2 dashes Worcestershire sauce
pinch of celery salt
1–2 dashes Tabasco sauce
black pepper

Pour the tomato and lemon juices over ice in a glass; add the vodka, then spices, and stir. Add a quick twist of black pepper. Garnish with a wedge of lime and add a celery stick.

*

Legend has it that this cocktail was created in Harry's New York Bar in Paris, France, when the bartender added spice to vodka and tomato juice (apparently, the celery stick was added later, probably by someone nostalgic for that grade-school science experiment). I prefer the (as yet unproven) theory that the Bloody Mary was actually invented by Mary Tudor in the 16th century.

Basic Eggnog
5 oz (150 ml) milk
2 oz (60 ml) desired liquor
1 teaspoon sugar
1 egg yolk

Pour the ingredients into a shaker with ice cubes.
Shake vigorously. Strain into a chilled glass. Garnish with
a dusting of ground nutmeg or cinnamon.

✳

Bahama Mama
$1^1/_2$ oz (45 ml) dark rum
$^2/_3$ oz (20 ml) 151 proof rum
$^1/_2$ oz (15 ml) coconut liqueur
$^1/_2$ oz (15 ml) coffee liqueur
4 oz (120 ml) pineapple juice
$^1/_3$ oz (10 ml) lemon juice

Pour all ingredients, except for the 151 proof rum,
into a shaker with ice. Shake sharply. Strain into a glass and
gently float the 151 proof rum over the top of the drink.
Garnish with a pineapple and a maraschino cherry.

Zombie

$1/2$ oz (15 ml) white rum
$1/2$ oz (15 ml) golden rum
$1/2$ oz (15 ml) dark rum
$1/3$ oz (10 ml) apricot brandy
dash sugar syrup
$1^3/4$ oz (52 ml) freshly squeezed orange juice
$1^3/4$ oz (52 ml) pineapple juice
$1/3$ oz (10 ml) 151 proof rum

Pour all ingredients, except the 151 proof rum,
into a shaker with ice. Shake sharply. Strain into a glass filled
with dry crushed ice. Carefully float the rum on top.
Garnish with a slice of orange and lime and a sprig of mint.

✳

Hurricane

juice of one-half lime
1 oz (30 ml) light rum
1 oz (30 ml) dark rum
$3/4$ oz (22 ml) pineapple juice
$3/4$ oz (22 ml) orange juice
$1/4$ oz (7 ml) maracuja (passion fruit) syrup

Squeeze the juice from one-half lime into a shaker with ice cubes.
Pour the remaining ingredients into the shaker. Shake well.
Strain into a glass with ice cubes. Garnish with a lime wedge.

South Pacific

1 oz (30 ml) gin
$^1/_2$ oz (15 ml) Galliano
Seven-Up
$^1/_2$ oz (15 ml) blue curaçao

Pour the gin and Galliano into a glass filled with ice.
Stir. Add Seven-Up to almost three-quarters full. Pour the blue
curaçao gently into the drink and let it sink to the bottom
of the glass. Then place a spoon into the glass, touching the bottom.
Twist it just enough to disturb the curaçao, which will
gently rise and merge with the Galliano. Garnish
with a slice of lime on the rim of the glass.

Cococabana

$^3/_4$ oz (22 ml) Midori (melon liqueur)
$^3/_4$ oz (22 ml) Malibu (coconut rum)
$3^1/_2$ oz (105 ml) pineapple juice
1 oz (30 ml) coconut cream
crushed ice

Place all ingredients into a blender with
a scoop of dry, crushed ice and blend until smooth.
Pour into a glass. Garnish with a slice of star fruit
(if you can find one).

Cococabana

South Pacific

Caipirinha

1 small fresh lime
1$^{1}/_{2}$ teaspoons brown sugar
1$^{3}/_{4}$ oz (52 ml) aguadente de cana (cachaça)

Wash the lime and slice off the top and bottom,
and cut into small segments. Add the lime slices and
the sugar to the glass. Crush the lime to make juice,
and muddle to make sure the sugar has dissolved.
Add dry ice cubes, the cachaça and stir.

Caribbean Sunset

1 oz (30 ml) gin
1 oz (30 ml) banana liqueur
1 oz (30 ml) blue curaçao
1 oz (30 ml) lemon juice
1 oz (30 ml) fresh cream
dash of grenadine

Pour all the ingredients, except the grenadine,
into a shaker with ice. Shake sharply. Strain into a glass filled
with ice. Add the grenadine, which will float to the bottom,
creating the sunset effect. Garnish with a maraschino
cherry set in the middle of a slice of orange.

Cuba Libre
juice of 1 fresh lime
1^3/$_4$ oz (52 ml) white rum
Coca-Cola

Pour the lime juice, then the rum into
a glass filled with ice. Top up with Coca-Cola.
Garnish with a wedge of lime.

Honolulu Juicer
1 oz (30 ml) Southern Comfort
^{2}/$_3$ oz (20 ml) golden rum
3^1/$_2$ oz (105 ml) pineapple juice
^{2}/$_3$ oz (20 ml) Rose's lime cordial
juice of one-half lime

Pour all ingredients into a cocktail shaker with ice.
Shake sharply. Strain into a glass filled with dry,
crushed ice. Garnish with a slice of fresh pineapple
and a maraschino cherry.

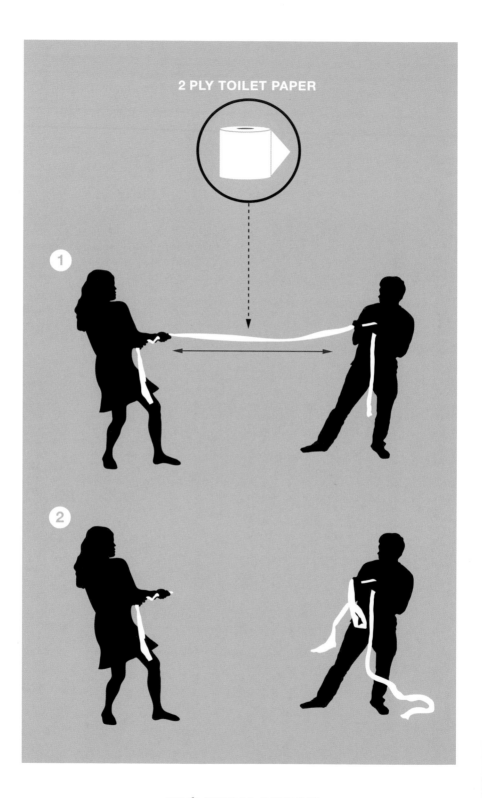

2 PLY TOILET PAPER

Game #8: Toilet Paper Tug-of-War

If there's one item hotels provide even more of than towels (see page 79), it's toilet paper. This ubiquitous modern convenience is dirt-cheap, it can be bought in army-quantity bulk, and it makes guests happy, which is why you'll find enough toilet paper in your bathroom to gratify all the elephants in the circus.

One of the magical things about toilet paper is a mysterious quality called "ply." Only the shoddiest flophouses stock one-ply paper, which is like wiping yourself with sand paper. Two-ply or more, though, means your toilet paper is suitable for a game of tug-of-war, either with friends (be sure to stand on opposite sides of the room for maximum effect) or by yourself. Simply tie one end of the toilet paper to the inside doorknob, then scoot over by the window and see how hard you can pull without breaking. When you're done, toilet paper the inside of your walk-in closet to let the hotel staff know how much you care.

Mai Tai

$^2/_3$ oz (20 ml) dark rum

$^2/_3$ oz (20 ml) golden rum

$^1/_3$ oz (10 ml) triple sec or Cointreau

$^1/_3$ oz (10 ml) Orgeat (almond syrup)

juice of 1 lime

2–3 dashes grenadine

Pour all the ingredients into a shaker with ice. Shake sharply. Strain into a glass. Garnish with either a small orchid or a wedge of lime.

*

According to legend, the original "Trader Vic" created this drink when he mixed together Jamaican rum, the juice of a fresh lime, a few dashes of orange curaçao, Orgeat (almond liqueur), and rock candy syrup. After vigorously shaking the concoction, he poured it into a glass filled with shaved ice and presented it to two friends visiting from Tahiti, who pronounced it "Mai Tai—Roa Ae," meaning "out of this world" or "the best." Or maybe it was Tahitian for, "Who is this crazy guy? Do we know him?"

Mai Tai

Mojito

1 teaspoon superfine sugar
juice of 1 lime
bunch of fresh mint, still on the stalk
1³/₄ oz (52 ml) white rum
dash soda water or sparkling mineral water

Put the sugar and lime juice in the bottom of the glass.
Add the mint leaves and muddle. Add the rum and fill the
glass with dry, crushed ice. Then fill with soda or sparkling water.
Stir. Garnish with a small sprig of fresh mint.

✳

Paradise Punch

1 oz (30 ml) Southern Comfort
²/₃ oz (20 ml) vodka
¹/₂ oz (15 ml) Amaretto
¹/₂ oz (15 ml) freshly squeezed orange juice
1³/₄ oz (52 ml) pineapple juice
²/₃ oz (20 ml) Rose's lime cordial
2 dashes grenadine

Pour all the ingredients into a shaker with ice.
Shake sharply. Strain into a glass filled with ice. Garnish with
a slice of lime and a maraschino cherry.

Apple Colada

1^1/$_2$ oz (45 ml) white rum
^{2}/$_3$ oz (20 ml) apple schnapps
1 oz (30 ml) coconut cream
2^1/$_2$ oz (75 ml) natural apple juice
one-half apple, peeled
^{1}/$_2$ teaspoon superfine sugar
crushed ice

Place all the ingredients except for ice into a blender.
Blend for 10 seconds. Add a scoop of crushed ice and blend
for 10 seconds more until smooth. Garnish with a wedge
of apple cut in three fine slices, to which you
add a maraschino cherry.

✳

Mango Colada

1^3/$_4$ oz (52 ml) golden rum
1 oz (30 ml) coconut cream
2^1/$_2$ oz (75 ml) fresh mango juice
one-quarter fresh mango, sliced
crushed ice

Place all the ingredients into a blender. Blend for 15 seconds
until smooth. Pour the mixture into a glass. Garnish with a thin
slice of mango on the rim of the glass.

Barcardi Cocktail

Barcardi Cocktail

$1^3/_4$ oz (52 ml) Bacardi light rum

$^3/_4$ oz (22 ml) lemon or lime juice

$^1/_4$ oz (7 ml) grenadine

Pour the ingredients into a shaker with ice cubes.
Shake well. Strain into a chilled glass.

✳

*While the Barcardi Cocktail should be made
with Barcardi rum, feel free to use whatever
rum your hotel provides. When your pickings
are limited, you can't be choosy.*

Planter's Punch No.1

1^3/$_4$ oz (52 ml) dark rum
2 dashes sugar syrup
1 dash Angostura bitters
juice of one-half lemon

Pour all the ingredients into a shaker with ice.
Shake sharply. Strain into a glass with ice. Garnish with
a slice of orange and a maraschino cherry
and a sprig of fresh mint.

✳

Planter's Punch No. 2

1 oz (30 ml) white rum
^{1}/$_3$ oz (10 ml) Cointreau
1^3/$_4$ oz (50 ml) pineapple juice
1^3/$_4$ oz (52 ml) freshly squeezed orange juice
juice of one-half lime
2 dashes grenadine
^{2}/$_3$ oz (20 ml) dark rum

Pour all the ingredients except the dark rum into
a shaker with ice. Shake sharply. Strain into a glass with ice.
Carefully float the dark rum on top. Garnish with a slice
of orange and a maraschino cherry.

Choco Colada
$1^1/_2$ oz (45 ml) sweet cream or milk
$^2/_3$ oz (20 ml) chocolate syrup
$^1/_3$ oz (10 ml) Tia Maria or Kahlúa
$1^1/_2$ oz (45 ml) white rum
$^1/_3$ oz (10 ml) dark rum
$1^3/_4$ oz (52 ml) coconut cream

Pour all the ingredients into a blender.
Blend for 10 seconds. Strain into a glass.
Sprinkle with chocolate shavings.

*

Raffles Singapore Sling
$^2/_3$ oz (20 ml) gin
$^2/_3$ oz (20 ml) cherry brandy
$^1/_3$ oz (10 ml) Cointreau
$^1/_3$ oz (10 ml) Bénédictine
$^1/_3$ oz (10 ml) fresh lime juice
$2^1/_2$ oz (75 ml) fresh orange juice
$2^1/_2$ oz (75 ml) pineapple juice

Pour all the ingredients into a shaker with ice.
Shake sharply. Strain into a glass with ice. Garnish with
a slice of pineapple and a maraschino cherry.

Sangria

2 teaspoons superfine sugar
4 oz (120 ml) Spanish brandy
1 oz (30 ml) triple sec or Cointreau
juice of one-half orange
juice of one-half lemon
1 bottle of Spanish red wine
one-half each apple, orange, lemon, and lime, sliced
soda water (optional)

Pour all ingredients into the container, beginning
with the sugar, then adding the brandy, the triple sec,
the orange and lemon juice, and then the wine.
Stir to dissolve the sugar and leave to marinate in the
refrigerator for a couple of hours before serving.
When ready to serve, add the lemon, orange, lime, and thin
apple slices. If you want to be more adventurous,
add fresh strawberries, blackberries, or raspberries for a
fruitier flavor. Hard peaches will soak up the wine
better than soft peaches. When the guests arrive,
add soda water to make it refreshing.
Serves 4 people.

Sangria

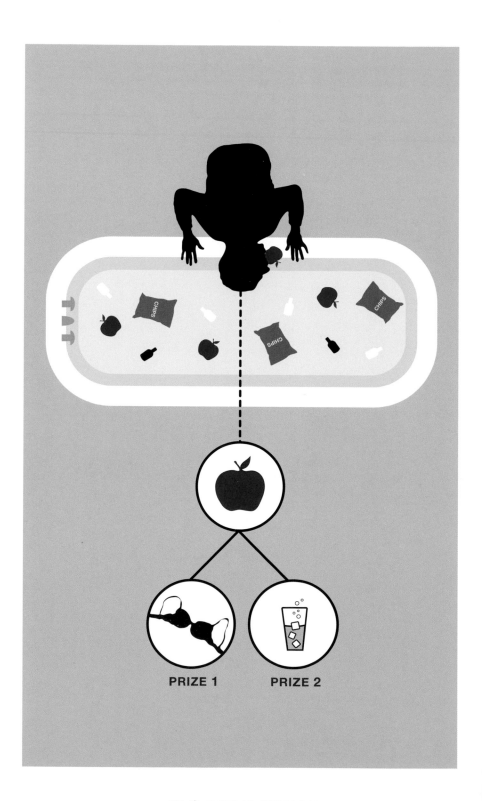

PRIZE 1   PRIZE 2

Game #9: Tub Bobbing

A generation ago, all the average hotel provided for its guests' bathing needs was a bar of scented soap and (if you were lucky) a small vial of some off-brand shampoo. Today's hotel bathrooms are like miniature outlets: You'll find skin creams, conditioners, bath beads and hair dyes, and if they threw in some makeup and a mud pack, I wouldn't be surprised. This hygienic largesse—combined with a sparkling clean, porcelain bathtub that makes your rusted old tub at home seem like a sludge-filled septic tank—cries out for a good, old-fashioned bubble bath.

But why stop there? You can use the tub for a fun game of bobbing for food: Fill a clean tub with water and drop in some unopened packages of pretzels and potato chips, then lean over the edge and try to dredge them out with your teeth. (If a fruit basket is provided, you can go the traditional route and throw in the apples.) Granted, soggy potato chips don't sound very appealing, but you can spice it up by letting the winner decide who takes what shot. Or, for the adult pair, perhaps whoever bobs out a soggy pack of chips can decide if someone has to take off an item of clothing?

Aquamarine

1 oz (30 ml) vodka

$^2/_3$ oz (20 ml) peach schnapps

$^1/_3$ oz (10 ml) blue curaçao

$^1/_3$ oz (10 ml) Cointreau

$3^1/_2$ oz (105 ml) clear apple juice

Pour all the ingredients into a shaker with ice.
Shake sharply. Strain into a glass with ice.
Garnish with a star fruit on the rim.

Blue Hawaiian

1 oz (30 ml) white rum

1 oz (30 ml) blue curaçao

2 oz (60 ml) pineapple juice

1 oz (30 ml) coconut cream

crushed ice

Pour all the ingredients into a blender. Blend until smooth.
Strain into a glass. Garnish with a slice of fresh
pineapple and a maraschino cherry.

Blue Hawaiian

Aquamarine

Beachcomber

$1^{1}/_{2}$ oz (45 ml) light rum
$^{1}/_{2}$ oz (15 ml) triple sec
$^{1}/_{2}$ oz (15 ml) lime juice
1 dash maraschino liqueur

Pour the ingredients into a shaker with ice cubes.
Shake well. Strain into a chilled glass.

Cape Codder

5 oz (150 ml) cranberry juice
$1^{3}/_{4}$ oz (52 ml) vodka

Pour the cranberry juice over dry ice in the glass, then add
the vodka. Stir well. Garnish with a wedge of lime.

Hot Buttered Rum

1 small slice of soft butter

1 teaspoon brown sugar

optional spices: ground cinnamon, ground nutmeg,
vanilla extract

2 oz (60 ml) dark rum

boiling water

Place the butter, the sugar, and the spices
at the bottom of a hot drink mug. Mix well or muddle.
Pour in the rum and the boiling water. Stir.

✳

Kamikaze

$1^1/_2$ oz (45 ml) vodka

1 oz (30 ml) lime juice

1 oz (30 ml) triple sec

Pour the ingredients into a shaker with ice cubes.
Shake well. Strain into a chilled glass.
Garnish with a lime wedge.

Margarita

Margarita

1¹/₄ oz (37 ml) tequila
³/₄ oz (22 ml) triple sec
¹/₂ oz (15 ml) lemon or lime juice

Pour the ingredients into a shaker with ice cubes.
Shake well. Strain into a chilled glass.
Garnish with a lime wedge. Salt the rim of the glass
before pouring the cocktail if desired.

✳

Now may be a good time to discuss the intricacies of obtaining a reliable lime wedge (or other fruit garnish) when your hotel room lacks either a) a fruit bowl or b) the kind of room service that can be trusted to send up thinly sliced ginger, or any of the other arcane ingredients these recipes call for. Truthfully, your best bet is to plan ahead—if you know you're going to be staying in a hotel with your entire marketing department, stuff some limes into your pockets before you get on the plane. You never know when they'll come in handy.

New Orleans Fizz

1^1/$_2$ oz (45 ml) gin
^{1}/$_2$ oz (15 ml) lime juice
^{1}/$_2$ oz (15 ml) lemon juice
^{1}/$_2$ oz (15 ml) powdered sugar
^{1}/$_4$ oz (7 ml) cream
1 egg white
3–4 dashes fleurs d'orange (orange flower water)
^{1}/$_4$ oz (7 ml) club soda

Place all the ingredients into a shaker with ice cubes.
Shake vigorously. Strain into a chilled glass.

✳

Tequila Sunrise

2 oz (60 ml) tequila
4 oz (120 ml) orange juice
^{1}/$_2$ oz (15 ml) grenadine

Pour the tequila and the orange juice into a glass
with ice cubes. Stir. Carefully top the drink with the grenadine.
Garnish with an orange slice and cherry.

Daiquiri
$1^1/_2$ oz (45 ml) light rum
$^3/_4$ oz (22 ml) lime juice
$^1/_4$ oz (7 ml) sugar syrup

Pour the ingredients into a shaker with ice cubes.
Shake well. Strain into a chilled glass.

Brave Bull
$1^1/_3$ oz (40 ml) tequila
$^2/_3$ oz (20 ml) Kahlúa

Pour the tequila and Kahlúa into
a glass filled with ice.

B-52

$^2/_3$ oz (20 ml) Kahlúa

$^2/_3$ oz (20 ml) Bailey's Irish Cream

$^2/_3$ oz (20 ml) Grand Marnier

Pour the Kahlúa into the glass first,
then add the Bailey's over a spoon, then the
Grand Marnier over a spoon.

Blackjack

1 oz (30 ml) Kirsch

1 oz (30 ml) iced coffee

$^1/_2$ oz (15 ml) brandy

Pour all the ingredients into a shaker with ice.
Strain into a glass filled with ice.

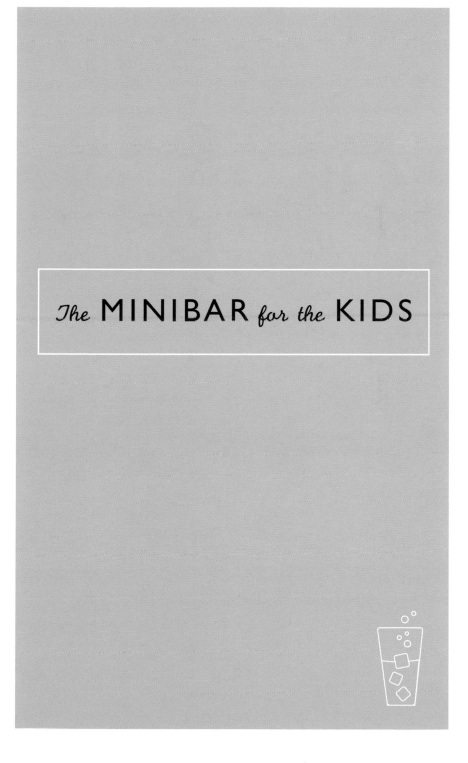

The MINIBAR for the KIDS

You usually go on vacation to get away from this kind of situation, but every now and then you'll find yourself stuck in a hotel room with a bunch of bored, hungry, fidgety kids, and unless you're a Cub Scout leader, the odds are those kids will belong to you. While it's not wise (or legal) to calm the tots down with a stiff Gimlet, assembling a non-alcoholic drink out of the ingredients in your minibar can be a fun family activity—as an added bonus, your seven-year-old can be the one to call room service for passionfruit juice, thus disarming even the crankiest hotel staff. Remember, you'll need a blender for most of these recipes, so make sure your room is properly equipped.

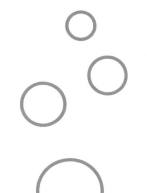

Apple and Orange Delight

4 oz (120 ml) apple juice

2 oz (60 ml) orange juice

1 oz (30 ml) Rose's lime cordial

Add all the juices to a highball filled with ice.
Stir well. Garnish with a slice of apple
and a slice of orange, if available.

✳

Coconut Grove

3 $\frac{1}{2}$ oz (105 ml) pineapple juice

1$\frac{3}{4}$ oz (52 ml) coconut cream

1$\frac{3}{4}$ oz (52 ml) fresh pink grapefruit juice

crushed ice

Place the ingredients into a blender.
Blend for 10 seconds and pour directly into a glass.
Garnish with a thin segment of grapefruit
and a spiral of orange peel.

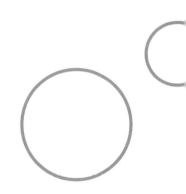

Virgin Madras

6 oz (180 ml) cranberry juice
2 oz (60 ml) orange juice

Pour all the ingredients into a glass filled with ice.
Stir. Garnish with a lime wedge.

Ginger Alert

3$\frac{1}{2}$ oz (105 ml) clear apple juice
1$\frac{3}{4}$ oz (52 ml) clear pear juice
$\frac{2}{3}$ oz (20 ml) lemon juice
small piece gingerroot
ginger ale

Put the apple, pear, and lemon juices
into a shaker with ice. Grate the ginger into the shaker.
Shake to let the juices soak up the ginger flavor.
Strain into a glass with ice. Top up with ginger ale.
Stir. Garnish with a wedge of apple.

Cracker

1³/₄ oz (52 ml) pineapple juice
1³/₄ oz (52 ml) passionfruit juice
1³/₄ oz (52 ml) cranberry juice
1³/₄ oz (52 ml) grapefruit juice
Seven-Up

Fill a glass with ice. Add the pineapple and passionfruit juices,
then pour in the cranberry juice. Finally, add the
grapefruit juice, creating a density of both color and flavors.
Fill the drink up with Seven-Up and stir.
Garnish with a slice of lime.

✳

Bora Bora

4 oz (120 ml) pineapple juice
1 oz (30 ml) fresh lime juice
dry ginger ale
dash of grenadine

Shake all ingredients, except ginger ale.
Strain into a glass filled with ice. Top up with ginger ale.
Stir. Add the garnish, if available, on top of the drink.

Bora Bora

Forest Fizz

White Sandy Beach

Forest Fizz
handful fresh blueberries
handful fresh blackberries
small handful raspberries
$1/3$ oz (10 ml) freshly squeezed lemon juice
1 teaspoon superfine sugar
5 oz (150 ml) soda water

Place the berries in a blender with the lemon juice.
Sprinkle the sugar over the berries. Blend until smooth.
Strain the purée mixture through a nylon strainer
or a fine cheesecloth into a glass filled with ice.
Top with soda water. Stir. Garnish with a selection of berries
on a toothpick across the drink, and a sprig
of mint on top in the middle.

✳

White Sandy Beach
$3^{1}/_{2}$ oz (105 ml) pineapple juice
$1^{3}/_{4}$ oz (52 ml) coconut cream
crushed ice

Place all the ingredients into a blender.
Blend for 15 seconds until smooth and pour the mixture
into a chilled glass. Garnish with 3 slices of banana
on a toothpick placed across the glass. Add a sprinkle
of nutmeg to finish the drink.

Cranberry Fruit Cocktail

3 oz (90 ml) cranberry juice
6 oz (180 ml) orange juice
1 cup plain yogurt
1 cup sliced peaches
crushed ice

Blend all ingredients until smooth.
Strain into two tumblers filled with ice.

✳

Cranpina

2 oz (60 ml) cranberry juice
2 oz (60 ml) pink grapefruit juice
2 oz (60 ml) pineapple juice
1 oz (30 ml) orange juice

Fill a highball with ice cubes. Pour the first three
ingredients into the glass. Stir. Add the orange juice—
it will sink slowly down the glass as you drink it,
but will look amazing at first.

My Mint Tea
1 bunch of fresh mint
2 pints (1 liter) boiling water
juice of 1 lemon
1 teaspoon lavender honey

Put the mint leaves into a heatproof jug and pour
the boiling water over. Add the honey and lemon juice
and stir to let the ingredients infuse. Leave to cool.
When cool, remove the mint leaves. Pour into
2 glasses filled with ice. Add a small sprig of fresh
mint and a slice of lime.

On the Beach
$3^{1}/_{2}$ oz (100 g) ripe yellow melon, diced
$3^{1}/_{2}$ oz (100 g) raspberries
$3^{1}/_{2}$ oz (105 ml) freshly squeezed orange juice
dash grenadine
$^{1}/_{3}$ oz (10 ml) fresh lime juice
Seven-Up
crushed ice

Pour all the ingredients, except the Seven-Up and ice,
into a blender. Blend, then add a scoop of ice.
Blend for 10 seconds more. Pour into a glass filled with ice
and fill with Seven-Up. Stir. Garnish with tiny
melon balls and raspberries skewered on a toothpick
placed across the glass.

Cherry Babe
4 oz (120 ml) orange juice
4 oz (120 ml) pink grapefruit juice
1 teaspoon fresh lemon juice
$1/2$ oz (15 ml) juice from maraschino cherries

In a mixing glass, combine the orange, grapefruit,
and lemon juices. Stir well. Pour into a glass filled with ice.
Add the maraschino cherry juice slowly and watch it settle
on the bottom of the glass to create a two-tone drink.

＊

Apple-Beet Beauty
2 oz (60 ml) apple juice
2 oz (60 ml) fresh beet juice

Shake the juices with ice and strain into a glass.

＊

Virgin Fizz
2 oz (60 ml) orange juice
nonalcoholic sparkling white wine

Pour the chilled orange juice into a chilled glass.
Top up with sparkling wine. Stir gently.
Garnish with one-half slice of orange.

Summer Sunset

one-half yellow melon
one-half papaya
one-half mango
6 strawberries
7 oz (210 ml) passionfruit juice
7 oz (210 ml) peach juice
grenadine
1 lemon
freshly squeezed juice of 1 orange

Scoop out the seeds from the fruit and discard.
Dice the flesh of the fruit so it's ready for the blender.
Put the fruit into a blender and add the passionfruit and peach juices.
Add a squeeze of the lemon and a few drops of grenadine.
Blend for 15 seconds to let the fruit combine well with the juice.
Then add 2 scoops of ice cubes and blend 10 seconds longer
to chill the drink. Fill 4 glasses with ice and pour in the liquid to three-
quarters full. The drinks will be pale red. The final touch:
float the freshly squeezed orange juice over the top of each:
The orange will sit on top of the juices, and gradually drizzle its way
in fine strands to the bottom of the glasses. Garnish each drink
with a small sprig of fresh mint set in the center
of a strawberry.

Raspberry & Orange Smoothie
5 handfuls raspberries
4 oz (120 ml) fresh orange juice
8 oz (240 ml) fresh natural yogurt
10 to 12 mint leaves

Rinse the berries and add them to a blender.
Add orange juice, yogurt, and mint leaves. Blend until smooth.
Serve in a tumbler filled with ice.

Considering the price of smoothies these days, this is one of the few recipes in this book that may actually be cheaper to prepare in your hotel room than to order at a restaurant. (Though that depends, of course, on the seasonal availability of fresh raspberries, and you'll either have to send your kids out to pick mint leaves from the hotel garden or do without). Come to think of it, if there's a fruit bowl in your room, you can create your own brand of smoothie—there's nothing kids like more than dropping random foods into a roaring blender.

Raspberry & Orange Smoothie

Berry Beauty

4 oz (120 ml) blueberry juice

4 oz (120 ml) raspberry juice

1 teaspoon clear honey

Combine all ingredients in a mixing glass with ice.
Stir well. Strain into a glass filled with crushed ice.
Serve with a straw.

Bitter Experience

4 oz (120 ml) fresh orange juice

1 oz (30 ml) fresh lime juice

bitter lemon

Pour the juices into a highball filled with cracked ice.
Top up with the bitter lemon. Stir.

Cantaloupe Caper

1 small cantaloupe, flesh diced

3 strawberries, sliced

2 teaspoons clear honey

2 oz (60 ml) plain yogurt

crushed ice

To make the cantaloupe cup: Cut a small slice off the
bottom to prevent the cantaloupe from falling over.
Cut the top off and cut the top edge into a zigzag pattern.
Scoop out the seeds and leave about $1/2$ inch (1.5 cm) of the fruit.
Blend all the ingredients until smooth. Add a scoop of
crushed ice and blend again for a few seconds. Pour into the
cantaloupe cup or a goblet. Garnish with a sprinkle of nutmeg.

Cucumber Cooler

quarter cucumber, diced

large sprig fresh mint

4 oz (120 ml) apple juice

Blend the cucumber, mint, and apple juice until smooth.
Add a scoop of crushed ice. Blend again for a few seconds.
Pour into a tumbler. Garnish with mint leaves
and a cucumber slice.

Coconut Affair

Coconut Affair

2 oz (60 ml) coconut milk

3 oz (90 ml) fresh orange juice

3 oz (90 ml) pineapple juice

6 fresh strawberries, diced

crushed ice

Blend all the ingredients except ice until smooth.
Add a scoop of crushed ice and blend again.
Pour into a glass.

✳

Coconut Cooler

6 oz (180 ml) coconut milk

3 oz (90 ml) milk

2 oz (60 ml) Half-and-Half

flesh of 1 medium coconut

2 oz (60 ml) sugar syrup

crushed ice

Blend all the ingredients except ice until smooth.
Add two scoops of crushed ice. Blend again for a few seconds.
Strain into four tumblers filled with crushed ice.
Garnish with a coconut wedge.
Serves 4 people.

Casanova's Virgin

1 oz (30 ml) raspberry purée
1 oz (30 ml) clear apple juice
nonalcoholic sparkling wine

Shake the purée and the juice with ice.
Strain into a chilled glass. Top with sparkling wine.
Stir. Garnish with 3 raspberries on a cocktail
stick across the glass.

As you prepare this drink for your kids, you may want to use the definition of virgin found in the glossary in this book—the definition of a virgin drink. Let the conversation about the other type of virgin wait until another day.

Casanova's Virgin

Frosty Strawberry Delight
3 oz (90 ml) pineapple juice
1 egg white
1 tablespoon clear honey
$^1/_2$ cup strawberries, diced
3 oz (90 ml) fresh orange juice

Blend the pineapple juice, egg white, honey,
and strawberries for about 10 seconds. Take the lid off
and add some orange juice, replace the lid, and blend again.
Repeat this action until the orange juice is combined.
Pour into chilled glass. Add a strawberry to the rim of the glass.

✱

Indian Apple
4 oz (120 ml) apple juice
4 oz (120 ml) unsweetened Lapsang Souchong tea
1 oz (30 ml) cranberry juice
Seven-Up

Pour all the ingredients, except for the Seven-Up,
into a large pitcher filled with ice. Add an apple slice
and mint leaves to garnish. Stir. Add the Seven-Up.
Stir. Serve in a chilled glass. Serves 2 people.

Papa's Papaya
1 papaya
1 small ripe banana
6 mandarin oranges

Peel the papaya, scoop out and discard the seeds.
Chop the flesh roughly and place in a blender. Peel the banana,
break into chunks, and add to the blender. Cut mandarin oranges
in half and juice them. Add juice to the blender. Add a few ice cubes.
Blend everything until smooth. Serve in large tumblers.
Makes 2 large drinks.

✳

Peach Passion
1 fresh peach, skinned and sliced
6 oz (180 ml) apricot juice
6 oz (180 ml) fresh orange juice
6 oz (180 ml) fat-free milk
1 teaspoon clear honey
crushed ice

Blend all the ingredients, except the ice, until smooth.
Add a scoop of crushed ice and blend again for a few seconds.
Pour into a glass. Add a sprinkling of nutmeg and a slice
of peach on the edge of the glass.
Serves 2 people.

Pink Velveteen

Pink Palace

4 oz (120 ml) pineapple juice
4 oz (120 ml) grapefruit juice
4 strawberries, sliced
one-half small banana, sliced

Blend all the ingredients until smooth.
Pour into a glass. Thread two small strawberries
on a cocktail stick and add to the glass.

✳

Pink Velveteen

3 fresh ripe figs
1 teaspoon clear honey
1 oz (30 ml) fresh lemon juice
4 oz (120 ml) guava juice

Skin the figs, slice them, and place in a small bowl.
Add the honey and the lemon juice. Muddle the mixture
until it is a consistent, smooth paste. Transfer the mixture
to a shaker with ice. Add the guava juice. Shake sharply.
Strain into a glass filled with crushed ice.
Place a fig wedge on the rim.

Game #10: Trampoline

Why do you suppose a hotel will, completely unasked, provide even the most obviously lonely and dejected business traveler with a king-size bed? It's not because it expects him to bring in an unauthorized guest when he only paid for one person to stay there. It's not because it cuts down on the workload of the housekeeping staff, or pares down the electric bill for that gigantic industrial dryer in the basement. Clearly, it's because the hotel expects you to use the bed as a trampoline.

As hotel games go, Trampoline is pretty simple. Your kids will already be well-versed with the game. Just climb up on the bed and jump up and down, preferably in full view of the mirror. You can pretend to be a spaceman, or a rodeo cowboy, or a race car driver, anything except an obviously lonely and dejected business traveler who needs to kill an evening because there's nothing good on TV. Just be sure to stash your minibar drink safely away on the counter, because with the prices your hotel is charging, who needs a carpet-soaking spill? And it's probably best to jump one at a time, so no one gets bounced off into the dresser.

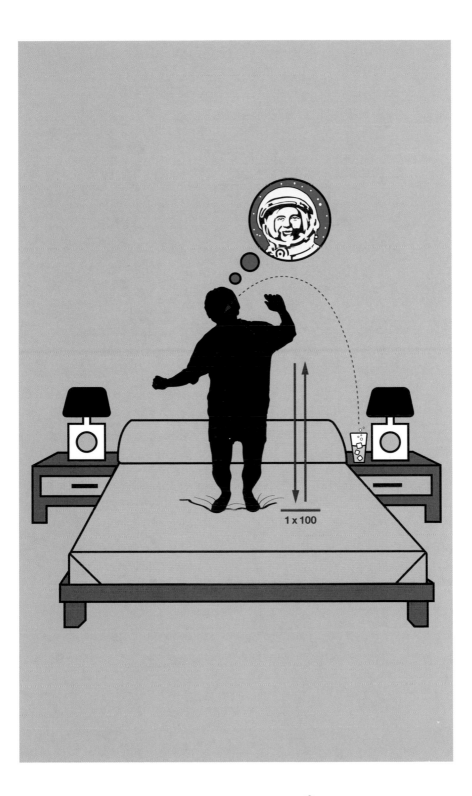

Mint Sparkler
1 bottle sparkling nonalcoholic white wine
10 oz (300 ml) apple juice
2 oz (60 ml) fresh lime juice
sprig fresh mint leaves

Place all liquid ingredients into a bowl with ice.
Stir. Add the mint leaves, taking them off the stem as you go.
Serve in wine glasses. Garnish with a spiral of lemon on the rim.
Serves 6 people.

Mocha Mad
4 oz (120 ml) milk
1 tablespoon instant chocolate powder
1 tablespoon instant coffee
1 large scoop ice cream

Blend all the ingredients with crushed ice until smooth.
Pour into a glass.

Raspberry Blusher

3 oz (90 ml) raspberry juice
3 oz (90 ml) grape juice
1 oz (30 ml) fresh lemon juice
$^{1}/_{4}$ teaspoon almond extract
ginger ale

In a mixing glass, stir all the juices and the almond extract.
Then place in the refrigerator to chill. Just before serving,
add ice to a highball, and then top up with ginger ale.
Garnish with a sprig of mint and 1 raspberry
on a cocktail stick.

✳

Raspberry Lassi

2 cups fresh raspberries
10 oz (300 ml) natural yogurt
3 teaspoons clear honey
3 tablespoons rosewater (if available)

Blend all ingredients with a few ice cubes until smooth.
Strain into four small glasses filled with ice. Drop a few rose petals
(if available) in the drink and add one rose petal on top.
Serves 4 people.

Moonlight

My Fair Lady

6 oz (180 ml) raspberry juice

6 oz (180 ml) white grape juice

6 oz (180 ml) pink grapefruit juice

3 oz (90 ml) fresh lemon juice

dash gomme syrup

In a large pitcher filled with ice, mix all the juices.
Strain into two highballs filled with ice. Serve with a straw.
Serves 2 people.

＊

Moonlight

one-half banana, sliced

4 oz (120 ml) orange juice

4 oz (120 ml) grapefruit juice

4 oz (120 ml) pineapple juice

2 oz (60 ml) white cranberry juice

strawberry and a mint leaf for garnish

Pour all ingredients into a blender with crushed ice.
Blend until smooth. Pour into two glasses. Place the mint into
the top of the strawberry, make a slice in the bottom of it,
and place it on the side of the glass.
Serves 2 people.

Shirley Temple

ginger ale

2–3 dashes grenadine

Pour the ginger ale into a glass filled with ice.
Add the grenadine. Stir. Garnish with a
maraschino cherry.

Singapore Swing

4 oz (120 ml) fresh orange juice

4 oz (120 ml) pineapple juice

one-half small banana, sliced

4 strawberries

1 tablespoon clear honey

strawberry and a slice of orange for garnish

Blend all the ingredients until smooth.
Pour over ice into a highball.
Add the garnish on a cocktail stick.

Orange Blossom Special

3 oz (90 ml) fresh orange juice
2 oz (60 ml) mandarin orange juice
one-half banana
1 teaspoon clear honey
mandarin segment for garnish

Blend all the ingredients until smooth. Pour into a glass filled with ice.
Add the garnish on the edge of the glass.

✳

Passion Fruit and Mango Cooler

1 fresh mango
8 passion fruit
3 oz (90 ml) fresh lime juice
2 oz (60 ml) sugar syrup
still mineral water
pulp from half a passion fruit for garnish
crushed ice

Peel and dice the mango. Scoop out the pulp from
the passion fruit. Place the mango flesh and passion-fruit pulp
into a blender. Add the lime juice and the sugar syrup.
Blend until smooth. Add a scoop of ice, and blend again for a few
seconds. Fill four highballs with crushed ice and strain in the
mixture to halfway. Top up with mineral water.
(Add less water if you want it to be thicker.) Stir.
Add the garnish on top of the drink.

St. Clement's
4 oz (120 ml) fresh orange juice
4 oz (120 ml) bitter lemon
orange slice for garnish

Pour the orange juice, then the bitter lemon,
into a glass filled with ice. Stir and add the garnish.

*

Great Grenadian
few slices fresh gingerroot
1 teaspoon clear honey
1 oz (30 ml) raspberry purée
1 oz (30 ml) peach purée
2 oz (60 ml) pink grapefruit juice
2 oz (60 ml) passion fruit juice
half a passion fruit for garnish

Place the gingerroot in the shaker and add the honey.
Muddle. Add the remaining ingredients. Shake well with ice.
Strain into a glass over crushed ice. Add the garnish.

Great Grenadian

Strawberry Field

6 fresh strawberries
handful raspberries
6 oz (180 ml) fresh orange juice
1 oz (30 ml) fresh heavy cream
sprig of mint
strawberry and a mint leaf for garnish
crushed ice

Blend all the ingredients, except ice and garnish, until smooth.
Add a scoop of crushed ice. Blend again. Pour into a large glass.
Add the garnish on the rim of the glass.

Strawberry Passion

1 lb (450 g) fresh strawberries
4 large wrinkly passion fruit
10 oz (300 ml) fresh orange juice
grated zest of 1 orange

Dice the berries and place them in a glass bowl.
Cut the passion fruit in half, take out the flesh and seeds
with a teaspoon, and add to the strawberries.
Stir in the orange juice and the zest. Chill for an hour
or so before serving in tumblers.
Serves 4 people.

Sun Grove
few slices fresh ginger
6 oz (180 ml) fresh orange juice
1 oz (30 ml) fresh lime juice
club soda
slice of orange and a maraschino cherry for garnish

Place the ginger in a shaker and lightly muddle it
to release the flavor. Add the orange and lime juices.
Add some ice. Shake well. Strain into a glass filled with ice.
Top up with club soda. Stir, and add the garnish.

*

Cookie Sandwiches
Package of vanilla wafer cookies
Banana

Peel banana and slice into
$1/2$-inch-thick slices. Take a banana
slice and place between
two cookies.

Sunset

2 teaspoons pomegranate juice
ginger ale
maraschino cherry

Fill a glass three-quarters full with ginger ale
and add ice. Add the pomegranate juice.
Drop the maraschino cherry in the drink.

Sweet and Salty

Bag of microwave or other popcorn
Chocolate candy pieces or gummy bears

If using microwave popcorn,
pop according to package instructions.
When popped, in popcorn bag, add
the candy pieces or gummy bears.
Hold top closed and shake
the bag to mix.

Virgin Sea Breeze
3 oz (90 ml) cranberry juice
2 oz (60 ml) fresh grapefruit juice
garnish of lime wedge

Pour the ingredients into a cup filled with ice.
Add the garnish.

✳

Ice Cream Sandwich
Package of large soft cookies
Scoop of ice cream

Order ice cream in the
flavor of your choice. Place a spoonful
between two cookies. Repeat
with any remaining
ice cream and cookies.

Glossary of Liquors

Although the foundation of every liqueur is a basic spirit, the diversity of flavors created through redistillation appears endless. Every imaginable fusion of fruit, nut, and spice competes to tempt your taste buds.

Apricot, cherry, and peach brandy are all brandy wines fortified with fruit nectar.

Bénédictine receives its slightly sweet essence from the infusion of nearly 30 herbs and spices into Cognac. Of note, Bénédictine contains cardamom, nutmeg, cloves, myrrh, and vanilla. The original recipe was given to Bénédictine monks in the 16th century. It's a choice after-dinner drink.

Campari is a liqueur established in Italy in 1860. Produced from herbs and citrus fruits, Campari is an integral ingredient in aperitifs. Campari's bright red color trumpets its presence in any drink.

Chartreuse's strong flavor is the result of blending more than 130 herbs and spices with wine. Yellow Chartreuse is milder than the green variety. The secret recipe for this liqueur was given to Carthusian monks in 17th-century France.

Cointreau, the prevailing brand of triple sec, consists of sweet and bitter orange peels flavoring high-quality brandy.

Crème de is a French phrase. It implies a liqueur with a thick viscosity. The word that follows de suggests its flavoring.

Crème de cacao gets its chocolate flavor from cacao beans and vanilla. White crème de cacao is, in truth, clear. It's milder than the dark (brown) variety.

Crème de cassis comes from French black currants, fruits, and berries.

Crème de menthe is a combination of mint and spearmint. Both green and white crème de menthe taste the same.

Curaçao is a type of triple sec made from the peel of a bittersweet orange grown in the Dutch West Indies. Its three color varieties, clear, orange, and blue, have an identical taste.

Drambuie is a mix of Scotch whiskey, heather honey, herbs, and spices.

Dubonnet is wine fortified with grape brandy. It's a popular, bittersweet aperitif flavored with several dozen natural ingredients including herbs, flowers, spices, roots, peels, and seeds. Dubonnet is available in white and red.

Galliano Liquore's primary flavoring is anise seed accompanied by vanilla, lavender, yarrow musk, juniper, and more than 30 other ingredients. An Italian product, Galliano's eccentric long bottles are easy to recognize.

Kahlúa tastes like coffee but expands with additional aromas of vanilla, chocolate, and coconut.

Maraschino's character comes from a sour cherry, called the marasca, aided by pure cane syrup. It's processed and distilled like brandy.

Pernod is a frequent substitute for absinthe. It's a secret blend of plant extracts mixed with distilled alcohol and water.

Sherry is a fortified wine made from white grapes produced exclusively in the Andalusian region of Spain. There are two major types of sherry. Finos are pale, light wines, while olorosos are dark, heavy wines. Sherry's wide range of colors and flavors is the result of different distillation processes and sugar content. Sherries don't carry a vintage date, as they are blended over many years from cask to cask. This maintains a consistency of flavor. Very dry sherry makes a tasteful aperitif.

Triple sec gets its name from a distillation process. Sec means dry. Triple sec means triple dried, or triple distilled. It's a useful orange-flavored liqueur.

Vermouth is wine infused with herbs, alcohol, sugar, caramel, and water. Although most people enjoy drinking fortified wines—such as Madeira, port, and sherry—straight, vermouth is highly mixable and a key ingredient in many drinks. Vermouth comes in four general varieties, although recipes differ from brand to brand. Dry and extra-dry vermouth is white, or bianco. Sweet vermouth is usually red, or rosso, but is also available in white. The last category, rosé, is semisweet. Vermouth is perishable and will spoil if stored unopened for too long. Unlike most liqueurs, vermouth requires refrigeration. As with bitters, use vermouth judiciously. Calibrate your pour to the taste of each individual.

Wine and Champagne factor in a few delicious cocktails. You don't have to purchase top brands when these ingredients merge with others. Reserve fine wines and champagnes for drinking on their own.